# Horoscope 2023

. . . . . . . . . . . . . . . . .

# Sagittarius

23 November – 21 December

igloobooks

# igl00books

*Published in 2022*
*First published in the UK by Igloo Books Ltd*
*An imprint of Igloo Books Ltd*
*Cottage Farm, NN6 0BJ, UK*
*Owned by Bonnier Books*
*Sveavägen 56, Stockholm, Sweden*
*www.igloobooks.com*

*0722 001*
*2 4 6 8 10 9 7 5 3 1*
*ISBN 978-1-80108-405-5*

*Written by Sally Kirkman*
*Additional content by Belinda Campbell and Denise Evans*

*Designed by Richard Sykes*
*Edited by Suzanne Fossey*

*Printed and manufactured in China*

# CONTENTS
. . . . . . . . . . . . . . . . .

# INTRODUCTION
··················

This 15-month guide has been designed and written to give
a concise and accessible insight into both the nature of your
star sign and the year ahead. Divided into two main sections,
the first section of this guide will give you an overview of your
character in order to help you understand how you think,
perceive the world and interact with others and – perhaps just
as importantly – why. You'll soon see that your zodiac sign
is not just affected by a few stars in the sky, but by planets,
elements, and a whole host of other factors, too.

The second section of this guide is made up of daily forecasts.
Use these to increase your awareness of what might appear on
your horizon so that you're better equipped to deal with the
days ahead. While this should never be used to dictate your
life, it can be useful to see how your energies might be affected
or influenced, which in turn can help you prepare for what life
might throw your way.

By the end of these 15 months, these two sections should
have given you a deeper understanding and awareness of
yourself and, in turn, the world around you. There are never
any definite certainties, but with an open mind you will find
guidance for what might be, and learn to take more control
of your own destiny.

# THE CHARACTER OF THE ARCHER

. . . . . . . . . . . . . . . . . . .

A sign that loves to wonder and wander, Sagittarians are the explorers of the zodiac, both in their minds and around the globe. Born in the ninth house of the zodiac calendar that signifies growth, progress for the sake of progress is not what this sign stands for, as the journey itself will be important to this meaningful traveller, not just the destination. The Sagittarian's quest for adventure, be it intellectual or physical, can be unquenchable because their element, fire, needs constantly fuelling to keep its flames burning bright. This sign can certainly shine brighter than most, ruled by the largest and third brightest planet in the sky. Named after the Roman ruler of gods, Jupiter makes sure that Sagittarians live with confidence and luck on their side; or perhaps it's not luck, but the hand of a higher being, as this sign can be highly spiritual or religious. Whether it's the good fortune of wealth, happiness, family, or faith, this sunny sign will find something in their life that makes them feel lucky to be alive.

Born at the end of autumn, Sagittarians are mutable and are perhaps the most open-minded to change of all the signs. Openness can breed honesty, which is perhaps why Sagittarians are commonly known as the zodiac's truth-tellers. Honesty is this sign's best policy, but their blunt delivery can sometimes need finessing. The Centaur Archer that symbolises Sagittarius can be an indicator of this sign's daring attitude and physical strength. With a positive energy that embraces physical challenges, Sagittarians can make fearless sports figures, like Eddie the Eagle with his record-breaking ski stunts. Above all, this sign can be an icon of inspiration, from Britney Spears to Winston Churchill, and at their core Sagittarians can motivate, bring joy, and encourage positive change.

# THE CENTAUR ARCHER

Mind of a man and body of a beast, the mythological symbol of the Centaur is one of the dual signs in the zodiac. As with any dual sign, like Gemini's twins and Pisces' two fishes, there are usually two sides to them. With Sagittarians it is usually divided, as their Centaur symbol suggests, by the mind and body. This sign is full of influential thinkers from William Blake to daring athletic personalities like Bruce Lee (who was also a known philosopher). The Archer signifies many of a Sagittarian's qualities: strong, daring, but perhaps none more so than this optimistic sign's ability to always look to the future. Sagittarians' aim can strike true first time, with the luck of the ruling planet Jupiter, or can dramatically miss. But fail or succeed, this hopeful sign is the embodiment of not giving up. The Archer can be dangerous, so risk-taking is usually common for many Sagittarians. As with any wild animal, the Centaur can at times feel restless, especially if they feel caged in any way. Sagittarians need to roam freely both in the mind and body to achieve their fullest potential.

# JUPITER

Ruled by the largest planet in the sky, Sagittarians are hard to miss. They are watched over by Jupiter, the ruler of the gods in Roman mythology, who ruled over the sky and was usually depicted holding his trident of lightning. For most Sagittarians, the sky's the limit and they will live their lives with optimism and the desire to broaden their horizons. The sky is an important symbol in many religions, and soul-searching Sagittarians may have a strong spiritual or religious faith. Jupiter is the fastest spinning planet in the solar system, resulting in it having the shortest days of all the planets, which perhaps explains Sagittarians' restlessness and desire to live each minute to its fullest. Jupiter is well known for having a red spot, which we now know to be a continuously raging storm. Whilst Sagittarians don't often lose their temper, this red spot on their ruling planet could be an indicator that when this sign is angry, it will be visible for everyone to see. Jupiter is associated with good luck, and with a daring fire sign like Sagittarius, fortune is likely to favour this brave sign.

# ELEMENTS, MODES AND POLARITIES

Each sign is made up of a unique combination of three defining groups: elements, modes and polarities. Each of these defining parts can manifest themselves in good and bad ways and none should be seen to be a positive or a negative – including the polarities! Just like a jigsaw puzzle, piecing these groups together can help illuminate why each sign has certain characteristics and help us to find a balance.

# ELEMENTS

**Fire:** Dynamic and adventurous, signs with fire in them can be extroverted. Others are naturally drawn to them because of the positive light they give off, as well as their high levels of energy and confidence.

**Earth:** Signs with the earth element are steady and driven with their ambitions. They make for a solid friend, parent or partner due to their grounded influence and nurturing nature.

**Air:** The invisible element that influences each of the other elements significantly, air signs will provide much-needed perspective to others with their fair thinking, verbal skills and key ideas.

**Water:** Warm in the shallows and sometimes freezing as ice, this mysterious element is essential to the growth of everything around it, through its emotional depth and empathy.

# MODES

**Cardinal:** Pioneers of the calendar, cardinal signs jump-start each season and are the energetic go-getters.

**Fixed:** Marking the middle of the calendar, fixed signs firmly denote and value steadiness and reliability.

**Mutable:** As the seasons end, the mutable signs adapt and give themselves over gladly to the promise of change.

# POLARITIES

**Positive:** Typically extroverted, positive signs take physical action and embrace outside stimulus in their life.

**Negative:** Usually introverted, negative signs value emotional development and experiencing life from the inside out.

# SAGITTARIUS IN BRIEF

The table below shows the key attributes of Sagittarians. Use it for quick reference and to understand more about this fascinating sign.

| SYMBOL | RULING PLANET | MODE | ELEMENT | HOUSE |
|---|---|---|---|---|
|  |  |  |  |  |
| The Centaur Archer | Jupiter | Mutable | Fire | Ninth |

| COLOUR | BODY PARTS | POLARITY | GENDER | POLAR SIGN |
|---|---|---|---|---|
|  |  |  |  |  |
| Purple | Hips, Thighs, Liver | Positive | Masculine | Gemini |

# ROMANTIC RELATIONSHIPS

· · · · · · · · · · · · · · · · ·

Like a moth to the flame, this fire sign draws lovers into its inviting light purely by being its dynamic and sociable Sagittarian self. Confident Sagittarians are not shy of taking the lead and braving it alone, but if they can find a partner to take on their endless journeys then they may experience their greatest adventures yet. A relationship that does not compromise their individuality in any way will be essential: a Sagittarian will not happily sacrifice their own dreams for others, like, for example, Pisceans often do. They will also abhor any signs of possessiveness from their partner, so Scorpio or Taurus lovers could be problematic. Sagittarians may have trouble committing to the one partner if they feel that the relationship is binding their freedom in any way. Learning to share their time and the art of compromising will be two tricky areas in love that this sign may need to work harder at.

With free-roaming Sagittarians, the grass can have a habit of always looking greener, and they may be inclined to eagerly wander from one relationship to another. If they want to find a long-lasting love that keeps the passions of their fire element burning night after night, then finding a like-minded intellectual or outdoorsy explorer to share their life with will be key. Air signs will not only keep this fire sign burning, they are also associated with the mind and ideas, so could make ideal partners for a Sagittarian looking for mental stimulation from their partner. A stimulating spouse is a must, as is finding common interests, which for this positive sign may mean adventures in the great outdoors like holidays spent wild camping and roasting marshmallows on a campfire. A sign that has a matching positive energy will have a good chance of keeping up physically with this wild Centaur. Fundamentally, this forward-thinking Archer could benefit most from an open-minded partner with whom they can see a future.

# ARIES: COMPATIBILITY 5/5

If Aries gets struck by one of Sagittarius' arrows, it will be a sure sign of Cupid's work. This couple's compatibility is high due to their matching positivity and lively personalities. Aries may have finally found their true match in risk-taking Sagittarius. With a shared love of travel, there's unlikely to be any Sagittarius adventure that the Aries would pass up on. These two are go-getters and if they can find shared interests then this partnership is an ideal match of two pioneering signs, the Ram and Centaur happily galloping side by side.

# TAURUS: COMPATIBILITY 2/5

Sagittarius is ruled by the planet Jupiter, which is associated with luck, something that a Taurean doesn't believe in as they value hard work more. Whilst a Sagittarian values new experiences, Taureans can prefer the comforts of what they know. The biggest struggle that this fire and earth couple may have is Sagittarius' need for freedom and Taurus' tendency towards possessiveness with their partners. A claustrophobic atmosphere should be avoided, and freedom generously given in this relationship. Learn from each other, admire the faster gallop of the Centaur and equally appreciate the steady plod of the Bull.

# GEMINI: COMPATIBILITY 5/5

'I love you just the way you are,' could be the vows of strongly independent signs Sagittarius and Gemini. Despite being both mutable signs that are open to adapt, there is unlikely to be anything about this match that either partner will want to change about the other. Being opposite signs on the zodiac calendar, the bond between Sagittarius and Gemini is usually going to be unique. For a sign that can become easily bored like Gemini, the adventurous Sagittarian is a perfect fit and will ensure this couple have endless days of love and fun ahead of them.

# CANCER: COMPATIBILITY 1/5

The homebody Cancer might end up feeling lost with the adventuring wanderer that is Sagittarius. Daring Sagittarians can help bring out a worldlier side to Cancerians and teach them that their sense of community can stretch larger than the end of their road. With Cancer, the roaming Sagittarius can learn the benefits of settling down in a loving relationship. These two have contrasting masculine and feminine energies that can complement each other greatly if their differences are nurtured rather than discouraged. Give each other plenty of room to be and reap the rewards from when opposites attract.

# LEO: COMPATIBILITY 4/5

With two fire signs like adventurous Sagittarius and spontaneous Leo, theirs is a love that will surely spark with excitement. Here is a couple that should keep their passports to hand as either one is likely to plan a surprise romantic getaway for the other with little or no notice. Leo and Sagittarius match each other with their positive energies and are probably the dynamic couple that is at the top of every party invite list. The philosophical Sagittarius and purpose-led Leo can share a powerful bond whose influence could be felt well beyond them.

# VIRGO: COMPATIBILITY 2/5

Whilst the outdoorsy Sagittarius and earth sign Virgo both have a strong love for being outside in nature, they have some serious core differences. Virgo's love for routine and Sagittarians' dislike of the same means that these two lovers may have their work cut out for them. The wild Centaur can sometimes feel too reckless for the over-thinking Virgo as they bolt heart-first after their goals, whilst a Sagittarian might feel that the Virgoan's overactive mind is slowing them down. Find some common ground, and this mutable pair could experience an honest and thought-provoking relationship.

# LIBRA: COMPATIBILITY 4/5

The good fortune of Sagittarius' Jupiter and the love of Libra's Venus could make these two lucky in love together. Fire sign Sagittarius and air sign Libra are sure to get each other hot under the collar with their complementary elements, helping to keep their passions burning. Both high energy positive signs, they should have no problem keeping up with each other's packed social schedules and will share plenty of adventures. The tactful Libra and sometimes blunt Sagittarius could clash if their ideas of commitment don't match, but they have a good chance of working out their differences and happily moving forward together.

# SCORPIO: COMPATIBILITY 2/5

Sagittarius and Scorpio can have a daring partnership: whether their gamble on each other pays off is another thing entirely. The adventurous Sagittarian will help expand Scorpio's horizons and appeal to their brave side, whilst Scorpio's fixed attitude can teach the flighty Sagittarian to stay motivated and see things through. The love of Scorpio can be all encompassing and the worst thing for a Sagittarian is for them to feel like their partner is at all possessive. This is definitely not a boring love, but flexibility and growth are both key for these two getting the most out of the relationship.

# SAGITTARIUS: COMPATIBILITY 4/5

An honest and awe-inspiring couple, these two lively Sagittarian intellects can have a fiery love. If any couple stood a chance with making a long-distance relationship work, it would be these two independent spirits. Two Sagittarian lovers will understand the importance of each other's independence so will be accustomed to giving each other as much breathing space as necessary. Their mutable natures make them flexible and ready for big changes in the relationship, whether it's moving to another country or starting a family. This is a pair that can inspire, spark, and dare one another to reach the highest of heights.

# CAPRICORN: COMPATIBILITY 2/5

A materialist Capricorn and dazzling Sagittarius can both be guilty of feeling a little superior, which won't do in a partnership, especially when these two can have different approaches to life. The rational Capricorn may be fearful of going to daring heights with their lively Sagittarius partner but if they are open to Sagittarius' optimism, they could learn to love more bravely. Sagittarius may feel constrained by Capricorn's constant reminder that actions have consequences, but looking before they leap could be a vital lesson for a Capricorn to teach their Sagittarian partner. The key to their happiness will be embracing each other's opposites.

# AQUARIUS: COMPATIBILITY 4/5

Placed two apart on the zodiac calendar, the positive energies of an Aquarian and Sagittarian can be a complementary and exciting love match. The thrilling ideas of a Sagittarius combined with the Aquarian's independent thinking can mean that these stimulating spouses will have plenty to talk about. The fire in Sagittarius brings an enthusiastic energy to the relationship and the fixed mode of Aquarius can help provide a focus to their ideas and bring them to fruition. Communal-minded Aquarius and sociable Sagittarius will likely be at the heart of their shared communities and bring great meaning to each other's lives.

# PISCES: COMPATIBILITY 3/5

The roaming Sagittarius and the escapist Pisces could end up blissfully running off into the sunset together if they can learn from each other's differences. Both ruled by Jupiter, these two may indeed have been lucky to find one another. Jupiter gives Sagittarians and Pisceans a zest for life and their shared mutable modes will make their relationship open to continuous growth and change. Pisceans can lack the active side that many fire signs have, whilst Sagittarians can lack compassion, which could lead to clashes with this sensitive water sign. Focus on common interests and this deep pair could go far.

# FAMILY AND FRIENDS

· · · · · · · · · · · · · · · · ·

Friends and family of a Sagittarian should be ready to get taken on a journey. Whether it's road-tripping down Route 66 or escaping to a meditation retreat, a Sagittarian can inspire both physical journeys and mental ones. Yoga mat at the ready, water sign and spiritual Piscean friends or family members can make the perfect partner to go in search of higher meaning and mindful enlightenment with. For more physical adventures, the active fire sign of Aries will rise to a sporty Sagittarian's challenge and race them to the top of any mountain. It's not all about the thrill of life that urges this sign on in their constant state of exploration: Sagittarians enjoy finding meaning in the world and what they do. As the charitable Sagittarian races over the marathon finishing line in their banana costume, their philanthropic Cancerian friends and family members are sure to be there cheering and offering their generous support.

A Sagittarian is a known truth-teller and sometimes their candid words of advice can be felt deeply by their sensitive family and friends. Whilst honesty is an admirable quality, the way in which Sagittarians deliver their wise words to their loved ones may need some work. Scorpio is a daring friend that may be close to a Sagittarian, and whilst the Scorpion is made of hardy stuff, any water sign has a sensitive soul that the blunt words of a Sagittarian should be wary of damaging if they want to hold on to their friendships. Expert communicator Gemini and diplomatic Libra may be able to help their Sagittarian friend word things in a more tactful way so that their words inspire rather than injure. The famous writer and Sagittarius, Dale Carnegie, who wrote

*How to Win Friends and Influence People*, shows just how influential the voice of a Sagittarian can be when delivered in a positive way.

Should the studious Sagittarius wish to start their own family, their love for learning will no doubt be something that they will want to pass on to their children. Sagittarians can make wonderful teachers, whether it's teaching their child to throw a ball or learn a new language. For the travelling Sagittarian, they may decide to bring their children up in a foreign country to truly broaden their horizons and give them their first taste of adventure. The Archer looks to the future, and as a parent the future of their children could be of utmost importance to this sign; planning which schools they will attend, enrolling them in sports clubs, and teaching them piano may all be things that the forward-thinking Sagittarian partner thinks about early on as they encourage their child to explore their full potential. As their children grow up, and even when they become adults, the Sagittarius parent will continue to try and challenge their children and impart their wisdom.

# MONEY AND CAREERS

Being a certain star sign will not dictate the type of career that you have, although the characteristics that fall under each sign could help you identify the areas in which you could potentially thrive. Conversely, to succeed in the workplace, it's just as important to understand what you are good at as it is to know what you are less brilliant at, so that you can see the areas in which you will need to perhaps work harder to achieve your career and financial goals.

Sagittarians understand the preciousness of time, remember Jupiter has the shortest days of all the planets, so they might not work well with colleagues prone to dithering. As a boss, Sagittarians can be inspiring, but they can also be preachy, impatient and downright mean in their critique. Sagittarians should try to appreciate that not everyone works at the same fast pace as them (Virgos especially like taking their time over projects) and what feels obvious to them sometimes needs to be pointed out to others. Sagittarians can continue to inspire by showing compassion and patience and always offering to help those that need help.

Clear career paths such as studying law, going to film-making school, or practising to become a singer could suit the Archer who has a clear aim in life. Caged within the confines of an office might not suit all Sagittarians, so finding a career that has travel prospects could appeal to this wild explorer. This highly sociable sign may enjoy a career that allows them to speak to the masses, whether it's as an academic lecturer who uses their intellect or a spiritual or religious leader who brings meaning to life. The most influential Sagittarians in their professional field, such as Steven Spielberg, Jimi Hendrix or Taylor Swift, are well loved because they have followed their dreams and help to inspire others to do the same.

The thrill-seeking Sagittarian may need to keep their wild spending in check and always use their heads when looking to invest or gamble their money, especially if they don't have endless funds to play with. Sagittarians may be interested in more high-risk investments but, being born in the ninth house of progression, they are also fans of seeing things grow. A more secure financial venture could bring equal satisfaction as they are more likely to see their money grow steadily but surely. If lucky Jupiter is shining down on them, Sagittarians may find themselves galloping to the races with an uncanny ability to pick out the strongest horses thanks to their inner Centaur.

# HEALTH AND WELLBEING

Whilst Sagittarians don't often lose their temper, the red tempestuous spot that storms constantly on their ruling planet of Jupiter can be an indicator of the outbursts that this sign can be capable of. The positivity of Sagittarians is a noble quality, however, this dual sign has ups and downs just like the rest of the world and cannot be expected to be all smiles. Learning how to release any upset in a positive way, whether it be through attending therapy, writing poetry, or trying out a boxercise class, is important for any sign and something that Sagittarians should not neglect.

For anyone that is prone to taking risks, they understand that danger is an inevitable part of the thrill. For Sagittarians, their physical activities may include hazardous sports like mountaineering or even being a stunt double. If risk is part of a Sagittarian's daily job or an aspect of their hobby, this sign may need to take extra care of their physical and mental health so that their body and mind can endure the extra stresses put upon it. Practising yoga and meditation could be helpful exercises for bringing strength and calmness to their action-packed life. If a Sagittarian is too restless for yoga, channelling the Archer in them could be a perfect way of satisfying their need for danger in the safety of a controlled environment of an archery class.

Sagittarians are usually sociable creatures and the life and soul of any party, which might have them out drinking and partying regularly. Over-indulging can be a problem for some born under this sign, and with the liver being one of the parts of the body that Sagittarians are associated with, hangovers could be particularly unpleasant for them, or at least that might be their excuse for staying in bed. Keeping a broad variety of friends will help a Sagittarian's social calendar have a healthier balance of partying and relaxation time. The invite for tea at a Taurean's house is just as important as the Leo friend that always has tickets for premiers or nightclub openings.

For Sagittarians that feel the Centaur running strongly inside of them, spending time outdoors will be of huge importance to their physical and mental health. For a sign that is constantly on the move like wildfire, taking a slow walk to soak up the wonders of Mother Nature could help soothe their racing mind. For city Sagittarians, reading their book in a park or signing up for an outdoor boot camp class could help bring them back to earth. Some Sagittarians may find that they have an affinity with horses and that the feeling of countryside air rushing past their cheeks gives them the greatest pleasure. If this sign is so inclined, horse riding will have the double benefit of bringing them joy and a level of fitness.

# Sagittarius

DAILY FORECASTS
for 2022

# OCTOBER
. . . . . . . . . . . . . . . . .

## Saturday 1st
Catching up with friends and relatives could be a good thing to do today as you may not be in the right space to pay attention to much else. Your presence may be needed by an elder or a person in authority. Don't try to force anything which doesn't come naturally today.

## Sunday 2nd
Mercury turns direct today and you could find yourself going over old ground once again. This may be an opportunity to check on details you may have missed during and before retrograde. However, this could be tiresome and leave you feeling like you've had an unproductive weekend.

## Monday 3rd
Social contacts could be at odds with you, which means that you need to find a workable solution to a problem. This could play on your mind today until you or the group are ready to accept something new. This will all work out fine if you group together to find an innovative solution.

## Tuesday 4th
Communications which are open and honest can put some new energy into existing projects. You could find a teacher who can inspire you to work within the boundaries that you have. Friends and interest groups can also be supportive and offer quality ideas, which could be moneymaking and raise your self-esteem.

## Wednesday 5th

Today you may notice that group efforts can make things easier than forging ahead by yourself. Once you've found the answer to a problem, fix it in your mind. You could find that you're getting emotionally attached to doing things by the book now and this boosts your confidence.

## Thursday 6th

Watery energy aids you in going with the flow of the collective. Family members can be a part of this. If you find yourself more inclined to be compassionate and patient with others, you may be rewarded with free-flowing unconditional love. Let yourself drift with this nice energy.

## Friday 7th

The little voice in your head reminds you that making permanent changes or endings makes space for new growth. You may now see a wide-open space in front of you. Don't be in a rush to fill it. Take time to consider the best way forward.

## Saturday 8th

Your inner compass is in sight and you may be amazed at how much it has shifted this year. It might be hard to believe that slowing down and looking at things from different angles has given you a more responsible approach to achieving your potential. This bodes well for your creative projects.

## Sunday 9th

Pluto turns direct now, and you could be looking at how much your value system has changed. What you've thrown in the cosmic waste bin this year is testament to your growth and maturity. A full moon showcases how far you've come in your creative and romantic pursuits.

## Monday 10th

There may be another deadline to meet today. This could simply be putting the finishing touches to a work project or finalising a deal you stepped back from recently. You may now see the benefit of holding back until the time is right to act. Get ready to rededicate yourself to your goals.

## Tuesday 11th

Your social life may get lively now as Mercury re-enters this area and needs you to have some fun and laughter. You can return to thinking about the simple pleasures you enjoy and how you give your time to others. Schedule some activities with your best friends now.

## Wednesday 12th

You may be presented with minor challenges today which can be overcome by thinking outside the box. Put your inventive side into action, but remember to keep it real, know your limitations and abide by the rules. Another mountain to conquer might appeal to your sense of adventure.

## Thursday 13th

Mental energy can set your mind racing and scheming again. Put this to good use and plan events for the upcoming festive season. Your friends and partner will thank you for your inspiration and clever ideas. Let your partner have their say today and, between you, a grand plan may emerge.

## Friday 14th

You may be stepping up and leading the way today, but if young people are looking up to you, be sure to be responsible and respectful. You may be hosting a get-together with like-minded folk and this can boost your ego. Stay modest and allow others an opinion.

## Saturday 15th

Your mental energy is high now, but is also at risk of being draining for others. Make sure that you don't get carried away with the sound of your own voice. You might need to tame it down a little. Gather your resources and enjoy a night of comfort, security and nurturing.

## Sunday 16th

Take a day of rest. You could be more tired than you think. Do something which can help you recharge your batteries. Try cooking your favourite foods, enjoying good company or deepening your interests with reading around topics which fascinate you. Feed your soul and you will be refreshed for the week ahead.

. . . . . . . . . . . . . . . . . .

## Monday 17th

The week begins with some challenging aspects from your mundane duties. Don't push too hard to rectify these, a solution will present itself if you listen to your intuition. If you feel vulnerable, understand that you may have exerted your mental processes too much and need more rest time.

## Tuesday 18th

You can be more outgoing now and have reset your natural default button which is filled with energy. You may have wiped the slate clean with a romance or creative idea and can pause before you decide what to do next. Don't repeat any mistakes you've made recently.

## Wednesday 19th

Stubbornness won't get you far today, but you might still try to push your opinions onto others. If your energy comes across as stroppy or childish, you may lose what you've gained, and this could knock your confidence again. Retreat and wait until this mood passes. Be humble and accept when you're in the wrong.

## Thursday 20th

Better energy brings you back to yourself and you might find that you can see more clearly. Your energy and drive have more compassion and what you desire now is harmony. From where you're standing – a place of passion and inspiration – draw upon others for their logic and reasoning.

## Friday 21st

A quiet day can give you space to work on your tasks without interruption or distraction. Be methodical and practical tasks can be easily mastered. You may have a way of helping others in the workplace which is valued. Be mindful of this today as respect will come your way.

## Saturday 22nd

A last-minute invitation can come as a pleasant surprise. Snap it up or you could regret it. You may think it's not your thing and won't enjoy it, but if you give it a go you could find it releases some pressure and lightens your load.

## Sunday 23rd

Saturn turns direct now. What have you learned about boundaries, communication and authority figures this year? You will have time to contemplate and play around in your psyche now as Venus and the Sun drop into your most private thoughts. Self-care and healing will be the themes for the coming month, so pay attention.

## Monday 24th

Your wider groups and social contacts ask for your attention now. It could be that plans are being made and they need you involved. As your mind and heart are in sync, you could accept anything that comes along as pleasant chatter and light-hearted interactions appeal to you.

## Tuesday 25th

A new moon and solar eclipse throw open a window of time for you to dig around in your psyche and look at what old habits and conditioning need to be healed. This will be easier than you think. Revelations can be catalysts for inner change which will lead to a more mature you.

## Wednesday 26th

You could feel some discomfort today, but remember that this is the irritation that provokes change and growth and is not to be feared. Don't make a return to your old way of thinking about authority today because it will undo all the good work you've done this year.

## Thursday 27th

Listen to your dreams today as you may get some insight about partners or friendships. There could also be an event which can involve everyone you care for. You might be willing to go the extra mile for others today as your mood is optimistic.

## Friday 28th

Jupiter retrogrades back into your family zone and suggests that there's something you need to return to there. An extra boost of compassion and empathy may be needed in dealing with some members. If you manage this responsibly you will be admired and thanked.

## Saturday 29th

Mercury joins the other planets in your private zone now. It could be the time to progress with your inner gold that you are used to hiding from others. What talents do you dumb down or have long forgotten about? Can they be resurrected now? Don't be afraid to showcase them.

## Sunday 30th

Mars turns retrograde in your partner zone. This can slow things right down but can also settle disputes or anything you've been questioning regarding your relationships. This might feel like stalemate energy where no progress is made, but you can also think about it as a pause and a time for review.

## Monday 31st

It may already feel as if an ending is upon you. However, with endings come new beginnings so change your mindset and see if it feels different. This may also be a quickly passing mood, so don't change anything yet. Simply sit with your thoughts and emotions today.

# NOVEMBER
. . . . . . . . . . . . . . . . . .

## Tuesday 1st
You might feel like the odds are stacked against you today. The niggles and disturbances in your psyche may feel too raw for you to deal with. Your role in your community asks a lot from you and you may not be in the right frame of mind to oblige.

## Wednesday 2nd
Be gentle with yourself and your partner. You could feel the first effect of the Mars retrograde this morning. Perhaps this will be a misunderstanding. There may be a revelation this evening where you come to terms with an old love issue. Let it go now and move on.

## Thursday 3rd
Smoother energy can make you deeply thoughtful and introspective. You may be coming to terms with what needs to be healed and feel far more comfortable about this process. Good memories surface alongside poor ones to remind you that not all of the past was a waste of time and effort.

## Friday 4th
Look at your inner compass now. You could see that although it's shifted, you are still heading in the right direction. Little or no action in your relationship sector is nothing to be concerned about. Remember that this is a time to pause and review things. Positive change requires a lot of patience.

## Saturday 5th

You might have started a low fire burning which is now needing your attention. This could be that you're going back to the roots of your romance or a passion for art. You could receive more insight into what you need to remove from your life.

## Sunday 6th

Do the right thing and act responsibly today. You can benefit by considering personal boundaries. A moment of realisation deep down suddenly makes everything clear. You might wonder why you've never thought of it before. Gossip or half-truths could make more sense now. Listen to your intuition.

## Monday 7th

Do your daily duties and keep your head down today. You may wish to lie low and not have to think about your personal growth now. A tricky conversation could mean that you learn something distasteful. Take time to process what this means for you, but don't let it set you back.

## Tuesday 8th

A full moon and lunar eclipse can close a window of wild card energy. This could reflect on your health and the things you value. Be on the alert for any subtle messages or signs from your deepest psyche as these can be signposts and show you the way through.

## Wednesday 9th

You may feel like rebelling or breaking free from the daily grind, but think twice. This could be a knee-jerk reaction to something you've recently discovered. You could be more aware of events in the past that you have wrongly understood and carried with you as heavy baggage.

## Thursday 10th

You might need to have difficult discussions with people, and this may be upsetting. However, this is a chance to put some puzzle pieces together and gain clarity over issues which have been rather fuzzy of late. In your heart, you may know that you've been disillusioned or kept away from the truth.

## Friday 11th

Don't be too hard on yourself for not knowing something that you do now. This is a strange concept to get to grips with, but you mustn't reprimand your younger self. Be mindful that you don't project this onto a partner. They can support you if you share respectfully.

## Saturday 12th

Step into your comfort zone and accept nurturing from others. You could be feeling exposed and vulnerable now and need extra care. The little voice in your head is still busy separating truth from deception and you may still be fragile. The dust is still settling on what you once believed.

## Sunday 13th

Deep emotions may continue to swamp you. Let them flow around you, but make sure you have an anchor and fix yourself to land. Think of this as an alchemical process which needs to occur. You could find that the unnecessary slips away and you're left with more clarity.

## Monday 14th

You could be taking back control now and feel better about recent revelations. Your mood lifts and you could be more optimistic. You may even be brave enough to stand up and speak your truth. However, don't be brash or pushy. Show others that this has made you strong.

## Tuesday 15th

It's possible that you could be more stubborn or refuse to be adaptable today. Others will just have to deal with it. You may be putting your foot down and making a bold statement. Just be careful as you don't want to cause more ripples. You need to be calm but firm.

## Wednesday 16th

Venus enters your sign today. Your personal strength can be tempered with self-love and you could be presenting yourself as strong and passionate. Don't stand for any nonsense or let people push you around. You may have seen through someone who has been duping you all along.

## Thursday 17th

Put your mind to different things today. Your methods of working and keen eye for detail can help you get through your working day. Mercury also enters your sign and your logical and rational brain will show others that you can be a force to be reckoned with.

## Friday 18th

Spend the day on your mundane chores and get your to-do list ticked off. Practical tasks can help you return to a sense of calm. By evening you may be tired and emotional but could have the time to relax and switch off. Do something quiet tonight.

## Saturday 19th

You could be in the right mood to grab your friends and organise a social event. In fact, it could be you who makes the plans. Get all your weekend chores out of the way then let your hair down. It will do you good to let off some steam.

## Sunday 20th

Catch up with people you may have neglected recently. A day of light-hearted chatter and connection might be the remedy you need to forget about upset and move on. You could find that an elder in the family is your best ally now and will know how to make you laugh.

## Monday 21st

You could wake with a renewed sense of purpose and wish to continue with the things that bring you joy. These could be your romantic or creative pursuits. There might be one last thing you need to clean up in the depths of your psyche.

## Tuesday 22nd

The Sun enters your sign today. This may be your birthday
month. Happy birthday! If you're still having an emotional
attachment to recent revelations, do something practical or
physical to get it out of your system. You should be able to
shake this off if it surfaces again.

## Wednesday 23rd

You may be close to your inner compass today but can view
it as an outsider and be more objective. You won't be fooled
again. You may now be more aware of when someone is trying
to trick you or dumb you down with excuses. Now is the time
to stand up and be counted.

## Thursday 24th

A new moon in your sign is a wonderful time to make goals
and intentions regarding you and you alone. Your ruler,
Jupiter, turns direct today too. This is an auspicious day and
what you set in motion now will prosper and bring you joy.
Mark this day on your calendar.

## Friday 25th

You could feel the effects of your recent traumas today. All
you need to do is relax. Don't try pushing forward or starting
new schemes and projects. Let yourself simply 'be'. This may
have taken a toll on your health, so take a day to unwind and
recharge your batteries.

## Saturday 26th

Your own home may be your refuge today. Sit quietly and look around you. You could be secretly plotting your next big project, but there's no rush to act on it today. Use your imagination and envisage what your home would look like if you had a clean slate to work with.

## Sunday 27th

Let yourself dream about doing something new. You may be considering a new fitness regime or a healthier daily routine. If you're in the mood to switch something up, try it out first. Make small changes, move furniture around and freshen up your wardrobe. Get creative.

## Monday 28th

Conversations can be light and cheerful now. Networking with others can give you food for thought. Write them down and file them away for next year. Remember that you're in the planning stages and the more thought you give it, the better the results will be. Follow guidelines and good advice.

## Tuesday 29th

If you've been seeking a teacher or guru, you may find them today. A person may appear who you respect greatly, and you may attach yourself to them as you know they have something to teach you. Your eyes and ears are open for anything new and adventurous.

## Wednesday 30th

You're being asked to merge with a collective or your family today. The lone wolf approach may not work well today, so stick with your people and accept the love and care you receive there. Sometimes, you need to remember that you're the product of those who came before you.

# DECEMBER

· · · · · · · · · · · · · · · · · · ·

## Thursday 1st

There may be some conflict or tension today. Your instinct is to put your own needs first and forget anyone who is disagreeable. However, it may be you who is being awkward. Check in with your inner compass and look at your actions objectively. You may just need to be more flexible.

## Friday 2nd

Your thought processes could be hazy now as you cling to a dream that is no longer meant for you. Find it within yourself to move on with an open heart and a willingness to learn your place in the wider world. Get ready, as romance or an artistic project could be on the cards this weekend.

## Saturday 3rd

You have sufficient energy to make a good start on issues that have been on hold recently. Tread carefully in relationships and keep all communications clear and precise. Your desires are there for you to obtain, but remember to respect all boundaries – yours and others'.

## Sunday 4th

Neptune, your inner compass, turns direct today and the fog will start to dissipate. You may need to have an inner dialogue with yourself and make sure you have an action plan. If you hesitate, it may be because you need to adjust, and this was something you might not have planned for.

## Monday 5th

There may be something you need to do within your family circle now. This could be a group effort which has been neglected or skimmed over. Perhaps you didn't know how to progress, but you do now. You could be surprised by how easily the answer comes to you today.

## Tuesday 6th

Speak to someone who can guide you up your personal mountain. You may have to deal with a financial issue such as an investment or a big purchase. If money needs to go out, make sure it's wisely spent. Large indulgences could set you back and trip you up.

## Wednesday 7th

Enjoy a reasonably calm day, but reach out and make important connections. You could be in need of a financial advisor or someone who knows what they're doing regarding home renovations. Gather your research and make a vision board. Plot your ideas before implementing them. Get the broader picture together.

## Thursday 8th

A full moon could highlight any issues in your relationship. You would be wise not to react to anything. Perhaps sleeping on it could give you a solution. You may have too many ideas floating around in your head. This is not the time to settle for one plan of action.

## Friday 9th

You might struggle today and could have a crisis of conscience. This could make you want to retreat into your safety zone for a while. If you need time to process how you feel, switch off from your duties and plan to nurture yourself. Feed your soul and your mind will be at peace.

## Saturday 10th

Today you can start building your empire. Venus has shifted into your values and finances area. You could get a better sense of what you desire and how to finance it. Good food and company are on the agenda today. Gather your closest allies for a movie and takeaway.

## Sunday 11th

You may have had too much of a good thing and wish to get back in control. Use the remainder of the weekend to do something you enjoy, but join the rest of the world outside your duvet. Your courage and high spirits may return by evening.

## Monday 12th

Learn from elders or people in authority today. You could be connecting with someone who can give you the benefit of their experience. Your community can teach you a lot if you step outside and offer your services. You can show your leadership strengths and may find a role that suits you.

## Tuesday 13th

It's important that you remember not to do everything by yourself now. Although you are capable of working alone, and often do, you need to fit in with the collective and take a minor role. This is a learning experience and will add skills to your resume.

## Wednesday 14th

Your focus changes and you can be more practical and methodical now. If asked to be flexible, you may find this difficult. Stick with working with your hands or making solid, long-term plans. A challenge must be accepted, but as this is no quick fix, you must dedicate yourself to hard work.

## Thursday 15th

Don't let your natural passion die down. People respect you for it. However, more earthy energy suggests that your way forward is by being grounded and focused. A new fitness regime could be what you need to fix yourself to a plan and see it through to the end.

## Friday 16th

Although you're quite happy doing practical work, you may yearn to get away and do something more artistic. Plan for time with your friendship groups this weekend and kick off the festive season with some fun and laughter. You could simply need to let off some steam with your social circle.

## Saturday 17th

Work may be on your mind, but you should use this weekend to unwind. If money matters concern you, rein in your spending and keep it simple. A discussion with a professional could help to put a few things straight. Think outside the box and accept any suggestions offered.

## Sunday 18th

You may resort to a trusted friend to help you think through your strategies. Phone calls and visits to people you haven't seen for some time can bear fruit. Be sociable but also pick others' brains for ideas you can build on in the future. Share your ideas with them, too.

## Monday 19th

You may need some quiet time as your cogs could be turning. Picking apart new concepts and rebuilding them for yourself could fill your mind now. Remember to put things down on paper or they could be lost, as your mind never fixes on one idea for very long.

## Tuesday 20th

Think about what skills you've acquired in the past that could be resurrected now. You may find that something or someone from the past comes in use. Deep thinking can produce something unexpected, but aligns with your core values. Keep it going if it suits your needs.

## Wednesday 21st

The winter solstice arrives today and gives you a chance
to pause and reflect on the year gone by. As the Sun enters
your area concerning property and values, it would be a
good time to seriously think about what you need to do to
enhance your life.

## Thursday 22nd

Put your personal dreams to one side today and consider your
duties to others. There may have been unnecessary tension
with a partnership recently, but you can remedy this by
planning for quality time together over the festive season.
Do something you both love and a shared dream might
present itself.

## Friday 23rd

The new moon is your opportunity to set intentions around
building up your empire and making it as solid as you can.
Bring together your practical skills and ability to see a project
through to the end. There's no need to set anything in motion
just yet.

## Saturday 24th

This is a lovely day where the planetary energy suggests that
home is where the heart is. You could be extra busy today.
Perhaps you're hosting the celebrations and making sure
that your home is welcoming. You can showcase your skills
and authority now. Add your own unique touch to the day.

## Sunday 25th

Today you may be more connected to your community than
you realise. Although you may be frazzled and have some
anxiety, you can stay in control by inviting your social circle to
contribute in their own ways. Your ruler, Jupiter, blesses
you with joy, optimism and abundance. Just don't overdo
the good things.

## Monday 26th

You might experience some inner tension now, but this could
simply be tiredness. You might want to leave any chores for
the day and come back to them when the party is over. Your
sense of responsibility to others is high and they will respect
you for it.

## Tuesday 27th

As the moon moves into your family zone you may think
you've had enough and need to do your own thing today.
However, you may be able to comply with requests for your
company and all will work out well. Nobody expects anything
from you. You are surrounded by unconditional love.

## Wednesday 28th

Expect a late surprise or two today as your responsibilities and
personal goals merge. By evening you should feel perfectly in
line with your inner compass and can rest easy knowing you've
done your best and those around you are satisfied. Reward
yourself with something you love doing or a personal treat.

## Thursday 29th

Mercury turns retrograde before the year ends. Remember not to commit to anything if it isn't to your liking. Try not to push your own agenda as you could clash with someone important and cause both of you unnecessary stress.

## Friday 30th

Take another day of rest and put all your plans on hold. You may not have the energy to do anything much and will be annoyed if you don't finish something you started. Go slowly with a partner as they could be feeling this too. Enjoy what's left of the holidays.

## Saturday 31st

The energy isn't favourable today. If you don't want to party, you don't have to. You could feel that someone is being demanding and will need to put your foot down. End the year doing what you want to do and not what another has dictated for you.

# Sagittarius

## DAILY FORECASTS
### for 2023

# JANUARY

. . . . . . . . . . . . . . . . . .

## Sunday 1st

The taboo side of love and money could raise its head today. This may require you to make a resolution that's final and shuts the door on the past. You have creative ideas aplenty in the areas of work and health. Whatever you begin today could start a revolution.

## Monday 2nd

Your gaze is currently towards the past, so it's not the time to line up big resolutions about your future. When it comes to money matters, wait until after the 18th before making a final decision. Explore new ideas with your family or loved ones and aim to help one another out.

## Tuesday 3rd

There's a buzz around ideas today as the planet of connection, Venus, enters your communication zone. This is great for brainstorming, marketing and asking for what you want. Spread your message far and wide. You could use modern technology and social media to attract a large audience.

## Wednesday 4th

Be a trendsetter in your chosen field and make your mark. Look out for people who are willing to share your ideas and join in with others to create a positive vibe. If you're drawn towards a good cause or want to take your sense of fun into the world, this might be your opportunity.

## Thursday 5th

Events at work could trigger a spontaneous decision regarding money. You could choose to go freelance or work part-time which could impact your finances. Technology is well-starred, especially if you run an online business. Ring the changes today and try something different.

## Friday 6th

Give yourself the weekend to mull things over and think things through. Today's full moon highlights your money zone and it's here where there may be a challenge. This is about your home and family and a situation that requires resolution. Consider how to let go of the past.

## Saturday 7th

If you want to talk to someone about money, an inheritance, savings or debt, line up a conversation or meeting this lunchtime. There's a little bit of magic around midday that could help you out of a tight spot. There may be some sadness involved, but take steps to move on.

## Sunday 8th

There may be a chance to settle a money-related issue this weekend. This may not take a traditional route and it could require some quick thinking on your part. You may want more time before agreeing to a job or a part-time money-earner.

## Monday 9th

When it comes to love and relationships, you're currently on a journey that began in August of last year. For now, you may not be able to get hold of the person you want, or perhaps someone's gone quiet on you. It's an excellent day to try and make sense of recent events.

## Tuesday 10th

It would be easy to turn into work late today, especially if you're not used to a new timetable or agenda. Once you're there, get your head down and be productive. You might be catching up on some learning. It's worth putting in the extra hours so you feel fully prepared.

## Wednesday 11th

Working alongside someone younger could bring the inspiration you're seeking. New people mean new and exciting ideas. It's a positive date to join a gym or join in with an exercise class. Remember that age is just a number and it's the lightness of your spirit that counts.

## Thursday 12th

If a partnership has been going nowhere fast or has stalled completely, Mars' change of direction today could turbocharge your love life, a joint venture or business partnership. It could signal a way in or a way out. Mars' passion can recharge your one-to-ones and get things moving.

## Friday 13th

Your best bet is to be charming today rather than overly pushy. This is where your strength lies. Negotiate carefully but cleverly and aim to smooth things over. This is particularly relevant regarding your relationship with a member of your family, an ex, or someone dear to your heart.

## Saturday 14th

It's an ideal day to get together with your friends, let your hair down and have some fun. Line up a pampering session, arrange a big night out, or organise a small party – whatever works for you. What's most important is that you relax, have a laugh and share any troubles.

## Sunday 15th

There may be plenty to gossip about today if someone you know has been breaking the rules. Try not to judge another person's behaviour and keep your opinions to yourself. It's a day when the less said the better. Slow down and take it easy.

## Monday 16th

You may not be back in the work saddle today. Also, it could be a challenge if you're having to deal with unexpected changes to your routine. If someone hasn't turned up, this will have a knock-on effect across the office. Do what you can without being taken advantage of.

## Tuesday 17th

When a lot is going on behind the scenes, it's never easy to focus on what you're meant to be doing. Do your best to be in charge or stay in control without adding an agenda and be clear about your motivations. This evening promises fun and games – in a good way.

## Wednesday 18th

If you're in any kind of negotiation or power game, don't charge in all guns blazing. The person you're up against may hold secrets and be willing to use manipulation to get what they want. This is potentially a turning point for money matters, but could flag up a loss or deficit.

## Thursday 19th

If you've been waiting on a payment or news around money, you can start to make steady progress now you know where you stand. Find the right people, say the right words and you can begin to move forward. Be aware, however, that other people hold a lot of power and sway.

## Friday 20th

The Sun's move into Aquarius today means it's a good time for communication in general. Promote yourself, your business and your ideas. This is your chance to get the airwaves buzzing, go viral and set new trends. Generate excitement at work and at home.

## Saturday 21st

A new moon is a promising symbol to start over and begin again. If you've been out of touch with people recently, reach out and reconnect. Use technology to make life easier. You could consider sending around a group email if you have lots to report to different people.

## Sunday 22nd

If you hear some surprising news linked to your work or fitness goals today, try not to let this distract you from other priorities. When it comes to community life, you may be stepping into a leadership role. Other people might want to listen to what you have to say.

## Monday 23rd

You may have to share some sad or disappointing news today. It could help to have a sense of camaraderie around you so you don't have to go it alone. If there's someone who needs your help or guidance, try and drop everything to be there for them. Do what feels right.

## Tuesday 24th

If you're still smarting from events over the festive period, make a point of sorting things out so you can let go and move on. This may be related to a gift or who paid for what. Line up a conversation or a heart-to-heart even if it's a scary prospect.

## Wednesday 25th

You may be acutely aware of the ties that bind you to your home and family, your past and where you come from. This means that the same issues could keep arising. Emotions run deep throughout families and you might want to let the tears flow. Line up something fun this evening.

## Thursday 26th

If you're typical of your star sign, you tend to look on the bright side of life and you prefer to consider the glass half full rather than half empty. This attitude may serve you well now and you can pass on your positive vibes to the younger generation. Action speaks louder than words.

## Friday 27th

The planet of connection, Venus, enters your home and family zone today. This combination feels sentimental and emotional. You might be taking a trip down memory lane or have big plans to find your dream home. Ensure you spend some quality time with your loved ones this weekend.

## Saturday 28th

Consider how much you invest in your lifestyle and your health. If you are eating unhealthily or not taking care of your body, make an informed decision to change your habits. Low self-esteem could stop you from spending money on yourself.

## Sunday 29th

It would be a great day to resurrect any New Year's resolutions that you want to give another go. This could be particularly important regarding your health and fitness. These are the key areas where you're wise to update your skills and change your routine.

## Monday 30th

It may be a case of third time lucky today. This is linked to success regarding a job or money matter. If there's something you've been aiming for since mid-December, don't be shy but pick up the phone and try one more time. Your Sagittarius eleventh hour luck could pay off.

## Tuesday 31st

When it comes to love and relationships, there could be anger or passion. It may go either way. What's for sure is that you're wise to engage with your one-to-ones and not avoid speaking up. In a competitive situation, it's a positive day to find out more about what's going on.

# FEBRUARY

## Wednesday 1st

You may be feeling wistful about a love that's lost or no longer available. Allow your emotions to flow and be grateful for the people who are in your life. If you're ready to meet someone new, it's an excellent day to join a dating site or initiate a conversation.

## Thursday 2nd

If you wake up worrying or you're feeling out of sorts, reach out to your best friend for solace or reassurance. Turn your attention to money matters and sort things out at home. Ensure your insurances are up to date and pay close attention to your financial outgoings.

## Friday 3rd

Someone close may be urging you to take a financial risk. You would be wise, however, to wait a while, especially if security is important to you. There could be a significant financial shift on or around the spring equinox. Money and emotions are closely linked. Invest in your safety.

## Saturday 4th

If you're caught up in any kind of financial situation, it's worth keeping on top of things right now. You may find that the pressure eases up towards the end of March. Do more of what you love later today.

## Sunday 5th

Today's full moon is perfect for going somewhere different and stepping out of your comfort zone. If you can get away or broaden your horizons, make it happen. It's a positive full moon for teaching and passing on what you know. New love could flow more easily than old love.

## Monday 6th

If you've extended the weekend into the working week, you're in tune with your stars. Your work ethic is likely to kick in later on but you may be flagging first thing. This evening, initiate a conversation with a family member to help them resolve a money or love issue.

## Tuesday 7th

Tempers could flare at work today if you and a close colleague don't see eye to eye. You could get caught up in a competitive situation trying to defend yourself and your reputation. Focus on the tasks at hand and don't waste time arguing or repeating an issue.

## Wednesday 8th

You may find out today who's on your side and who's not. It's never easy when you have different personalities vying to be heard, especially when there are conflicting opinions. Turn to a member of your family for reassurance. A friend who's a tech wizard could prove to be a godsend.

## Thursday 9th

Turn to your friends if you're seeking a non-biased opinion. Whether you're talking about money, love or a work situation, it's important to have an objective view from someone who's not closely involved. There are always two sides to every coin, so be impartial where possible.

## Friday 10th

If you're in a situation, this weekend is pivotal. You could decide to cut your losses so you can move on. Consider what's working out for you financially and what's not. Lay down the law with someone younger in your life and refuse to keep paying out.

## Saturday 11th

There's a lively vibe going on this weekend and this is your cue to start socialising more and get out and about in your local community. People count and it's a great time for new connections and making friends. It's a positive weekend for study and gaining knowledge.

## Sunday 12th

You could feel worn out today and may need to put your feet up and take it easy. Your plans to catch up on correspondence could go out of the window. Do what feels right for you and turn your attention inwards. If you have a spiritual soul, reconnect with your faith.

## Monday 13th

If you're still feeling upset over a recent conversation, try and let it go. Going back over things won't help and it's not the time to resolve a personal situation. Take a step back and slow things down. You'll need all your energy for the excitement over the next few days.

## Tuesday 14th

It's Valentine's Day and the moon is in your star sign, which puts you in the cosmic spotlight. Plus, your ruling planet, Jupiter, could sprinkle some Valentine's Day luck and romance your way. If you're looking for love, sign up for a singles event this evening.

## Wednesday 15th

Don't worry if someone special forgot to treat you yesterday. Today looks gorgeous for a romantic occasion, especially at midday. Forgive and forget and you can enjoy some quality time together. Bond closely with the one you love or take a step closer towards finding your dream home.

## Thursday 16th

It would be a good day to have a serious conversation. You might, however, want to stay quiet because you're not informed or you need to do more research. You may be undergoing a period of intense study and have commitments that require you to step up.

## Friday 17th

Whatever's in store for you, ensure you stay on the straight and narrow when it comes to spending, saving and investing. Look to your long-term future and don't get involved with anything corrupt or illegal. You may have to work smart, not hard, to ensure your money is safe.

## Saturday 18th

This weekend's astrology could be disorienting at times. This is because you're a future-oriented person and at your best when you can look ahead. However, the Sun's move into your home and family zone today is tugging at your emotions and returns your attention towards the past.

## Sunday 19th

You could be feeling rootless and not settled or secure. If there's been an ongoing issue with a sibling or neighbour, it would be a good day to try and clear up a misunderstanding. A new moon is on the way which is ideal for starting over with people close to you.

## Monday 20th

A new moon in your home and family zone is the ideal time to forgive and start afresh. Also, love planet Venus moves into fire sign Aries, which is less emotional and more passionate. This is the start of a lively couple of months when you're wise to enjoy all the good things in life.

## Tuesday 21st

It could be harder to communicate with family members or the people you share your life with today. Nothing is clear or set in stone, so assume nothing and keep your options open. A minor issue this evening could blow up out of all proportion if you speak out of turn.

## Wednesday 22nd

Today's astrology is gorgeous for you. It could be romantic or joyful, creative or playful. Make the most of the best two planets, Venus and Jupiter, in your good times zone. Hang out with your kids or ask someone out on a date. Be bold and daring in your close relationships.

## Thursday 23rd

It's a lively period for love and relationships so make the most of it. Initiate a conversation with someone you meet when you're out and about or line up a spontaneous date with your other half. Look out for an expert with advice that could save you time and money.

## Friday 24th

If you're struggling to catch up at work, it's a good day to slow things down rather than keep pushing. You could benefit from an extra pair of hands to help you or a more efficient system, either at work or at home. Streamline your work to achieve maximum productivity.

## Saturday 25th

Turn your attention to your health and fitness. It would be an excellent day to leap into a new exercise routine or start a healthy eating regime, whatever works for you. The key is to be spontaneous and not think about it too much. Even a small change to your lifestyle could benefit you.

## Sunday 26th

Someone is likely to disagree with you today, especially if you're talking about anything alternative, new age or controversial. That doesn't mean you're not right, but allow other people to have their opinion. A chinwag with your favourite person could help put the world to rights.

## Monday 27th

You have some passionate stars boosting your love life.
If you're in a relationship, it's the little things that count
and make the most difference. Keep love alive by reminding
yourself and the one you love of all the good times you've
shared.

## Tuesday 28th

You know you're with the right person when they make your
life better not worse. Ask for more compliments if you want
them. Be articulate and direct in your communications. Your
enthusiasm is infectious. You could make someone's day extra
special when you reach out to them.

# MARCH
··················

### Wednesday 1st
Try not to fixate on what's not working out. Instead, turn your attention to problem-solving and fix an ongoing issue. When you waste too much energy complaining, this leaves no space for positive ideas to flourish and grow. Channel any worry or anxiety into a constructive solution.

### Thursday 2nd
Communication planet Mercury moves into your home and family zone today. This could be a sentimental or emotional time when you're drawn back towards the past or you're dealing with a family issue. It is, however, one of the best days for love and romance all year, so make the most of it.

### Friday 3rd
Don't leave anything unattended at home or regarding your family. Have those all-important conversations and get any jobs handled. If there's a cash deficit or someone close is struggling to pay the bills, be supportive rather than judge them harshly. A weekend away would be ideal.

### Saturday 4th
This is a lovely weekend for being on holiday or going somewhere completely different. If you want to revive a relationship or treat a new love interest, make a special effort over the next few days. It's a time when love and feel-good vibes are in the ascendancy.

## Sunday 5th

Line up an adventure or a day out. Ideally, you'll be somewhere exotic but if not, make the most of life closer to home. You might be at a music event or a personal growth workshop. Whatever you're doing, make sure it expands your life experience for the better.

## Monday 6th

You may be craving security more than usual now, or you want everything to be straightforward in life. With live-wire planet Uranus lighting up your work and lifestyle zone, however, anything goes. You may prefer to work from home or change your routine to suit you.

## Tuesday 7th

Today's full moon falls across the foundations of your horoscope. This is about your career and where you're heading in life. If you're disillusioned with your current path, trust your intuition as it's telling you something important about what is next. Deal with the facts and trust yourself.

## Wednesday 8th

If you're confined to home, try not to feel disheartened and be kind to yourself. You may be keen to build new foundations and be ready to settle down rather than keep moving. When it comes to your home and your family, you're being urged to get real and decide what comes next.

## Thursday 9th

If you're typical of your star sign, you have plenty of enthusiasm and a desire for adventure. If you're trying to get your friends enthusiastic about joining you in a new experience, you might have to work extra hard to get them involved. Be careful that you don't get overexcited.

## Friday 10th

If you're involved in a group project, it's important to let everyone have their say. You could find out what's really going on as something hidden may be revealed. If you're out on the town this evening, take good care of your purse or belongings. Decide on your budget before leaving home.

## Saturday 11th

If you'd benefit from some quiet time this weekend, make a commitment to prioritise self-care. A loving relationship could put a smile on your face as long things don't get too over-complicated. When your body needs a rest, it's wise to listen to your inner voice.

## Sunday 12th

If you've got a big week coming up, be sensible today and prioritise your wellbeing. It would be a lovely day for some rest and relaxation or some pampering. Sometimes, you have to actively stop and slow down to reconnect with your inner compass. Adopt a spiritual practice today.

## Monday 13th

The moon's back in your star sign. This is a great way to start the week as you can take centre stage. If you've been at home all weekend, you might be ready to get back in the hustle and bustle of life. Do take your responsibilities seriously, especially with a parent.

## Tuesday 14th

Keep your wits about you and don't allow yourself to be persuaded or seduced. You may find out about a scandal or change your mind about someone based on what you hear. Go with the flow when it comes to love. This is not the time to try and make sense of things.

## Wednesday 15th

You may be feeling more emotional and sensitive than usual over the next couple of days. If you're grieving the past or immersed in your memories, allow yourself to express your emotions fully. Choose your allies carefully and keep your trust antennae on high alert.

## Thursday 16th

When it comes to money, sometimes you have to do less not more. Notice where you might need to cut back or minimise expenses. This is a good time to concentrate on the necessities of life. Focus on the basics and be diligent about your work and your health.

## Friday 17th

If you're a typical Sagittarius, you don't always enjoy a daily routine. However, this could benefit you now if you want to be healthy in your mind, body and soul. When you look after yourself on a regular basis, this can help you in other ways too. Make your peace within the family.

## Saturday 18th

Work your connections this weekend. They can help you, especially people you know through your work or in your daily life. Someone close could offer you an innovative or clever idea. If so, follow it up, talk things through and work things out together. Be thorough in your approach.

## Sunday 19th

If there's something important that you want to confront or talk about, go for it today. Don't shy away from a taboo issue and be direct and honest about your wants and needs. If you're a parent, it might be a good time to tackle a tricky conversation. Don't leave things unsaid.

## Monday 20th

The Sun's move into Aries today could be a glowing beacon for you. It falls in your creativity zone and this includes play and having fun. It's the perfect time to line up some entertainment, whether with the kids, a new lover, your friends or your family.

## Tuesday 21st

Romance is part and parcel of today's new moon in Aries. It's an excellent date to declare your intentions. Be open to all things new and be loving and giving. Be clear about what you want and say it out loud to the universe. The new moon can be a powerful manifesting tool.

## Wednesday 22nd

Be around the people in your life who make you laugh and remind you of all the good things happening out in the world. Gather your loved ones around you and throw a party or celebration. There are some serious feel-good vibes taking place. It's a lucky time, so it might be the right time to take a chance.

## Thursday 23rd

You could experience a financial breakthrough today as a challenging period comes to an end. You may need to stand your ground or speak your mind, but be aware that words have power and can be used as a weapon. Wield your power effectively but thoughtfully.

## Friday 24th

Don't take matters for granted and pay close attention to what's happening. You may hear news of a job or a fitness routine that's right for you. Use the internet to speed up your progress. It could be time to think about an alternative job or lifestyle, something more in tune with who you are.

## Saturday 25th

Money becomes important from today onwards as action planet Mars enters your joint finance zone. You may have no option but to be more forthright and determined around money. However, the key to your success is not to go it alone. Get the right kind of help and advice.

## Sunday 26th

Make time for loved ones today and prioritise your close relationships. It's easy to get caught up with chores or lose yourself in everyday tasks. A parent could require more of your attention. Find the joy wherever you can in your life.

## Monday 27th

Be around the right people today and you'll soon be laughing wholeheartedly. It might be the start of the working week, but it's the people in your life who count. Make time for the kids, hang out with a lover, engage with your work colleagues. Good news might be a welcome bonus.

## Tuesday 28th

You might enjoy hanging out with your children or contacting your grandchildren today. You may be ready to inject energy into your life or to lift people's spirits. Focus on life in the here and now and make the most of simple pleasures. This is potentially a lucky period.

## Wednesday 29th

Work is under the cosmic spotlight today. Consider how to keep your income steady and your outgoings stable without taking away too much fun. If a regular job comes up, say yes. If you find a way to monitor your spending more closely, go for it. Do whatever it takes to feel secure.

## Thursday 30th

It's via your work that there may be an opportunity to stabilise your finances. Take the sensible work option or apply for a new job. Technology could help too, so use it to your advantage. Listen to a work colleague whose crazy ideas could be worth following up.

## Friday 31st

Book a last-minute trip away or go and visit a friend who lives out of town. Make sure you enjoy the weekend to the full and don't get caught up with work or responsibilities. It's easy to lose yourself in the mundane but that won't boost your spirits or put a smile on your face.

# APRIL
·················

## Saturday 1st

Your zodiac archetype is the explorer. This means you need
more than your fair share of adventure and new experiences if
you're typical of your star sign. Make the most of life now and
line up some new goals for the future. Fire your arrows high
into the sky to see where they land.

## Sunday 2nd

You could get pulled back into the world of work today, or
perhaps you've recently taken on a position of responsibility
that requires your time and focus. Try not to let a situation
at home or within your family get you down. Engage actively
with others and be a tight-knit unit.

## Monday 3rd

Communication planet Mercury enters your work and health
zone today. Prioritise these areas of life and take good care of
yourself. This is especially important if things aren't working
out the way you want them to, or perhaps you have a difficult
conversation that depletes your energy.

## Tuesday 4th

You may be feeling tired from spending too much time online.
Be flexible and keep on your toes if life is busy. There could
be unexpected demands that crop up and a certain amount
of change or flow is required. This is where your mutable,
adaptable nature can be helpful.

## Wednesday 5th

The moon is in your friendship zone today but you may find it a challenge to leave work behind and fit in some socialising. It looks as if you have a lot to pay attention to and working hard could pay dividends. This is especially important if you want to address a financial situation.

## Thursday 6th

The full moon highlights the social axis of your horoscope. You may experience a revelation about friends, your children or a lover and want to engage with them more fully. Find ways to celebrate life and do more of what you love. Reach out to someone special and let them know you care.

## Friday 7th

If you were out partying last night on the full moon, you'll be keen to take things slowly today. Try not to overreact to other people and keep your relationships amicable. A drink with a work colleague could prove meaningful, especially when they reveal more about their home life.

## Saturday 8th

It may be Easter weekend, but you could choose to have a productive time. If you want to catch up with work or finances, crack on with things today. You may have some clever ideas about how to make these key areas of your life run smoother. Have a nap when you need one.

## Sunday 9th

There's no rush and you'll enjoy lounging around first thing and taking it easy. If you have strong faith, reconnect with your spiritual or religious nature on this important day. The moon's move into your star sign at lunchtime livens things up immensely. Find your place to shine.

## Monday 10th

Today, do what feels right for you. There may be no opposition to your plans and you could have a high level of self-awareness. It may feel important for you to be true to who you are and express yourself honestly. This is one of your strengths so use it wisely.

## Tuesday 11th

Today's Sun-Jupiter conjunction is gorgeous for you as it falls in the pleasure zone of your horoscope. This is a heady combination and the perfect excuse to do more of what you love. As Venus enters your relationship zone too, romance could be at an all-time high.

## Wednesday 12th

You may be glowing from the aftermath of yesterday's Sun-Jupiter connection. Perhaps you met someone special. Today's events could, however, bring you back down to earth with a bump and money – or lack of it – is the likely culprit.

## Thursday 13th

Your money values might be changing. You may have an opportunity to take what you've learned or discovered about money into the world. This might mean making a conscious decision about where you invest or spend your money or how to deal with debt.

. . . . . . . . . . . . . . . . .

## Friday 14th

Love might not work out the way you want today, or perhaps it's easy to slip into negativity and you might feel sad about a loss or bereavement. Try not to let recent events frustrate or disappoint you. Choose carefully who you spend your time with.

## Saturday 15th

Be around the people in your life you know and trust, the ones you can rely on for good banter and positive vibes. This might be your children, a lover or your best friend. It's an excellent day to enjoy a party or get-together, especially if you want to meet new people.

## Sunday 16th

Deal with any financial or family matters first thing. Get the more challenging stuff out of the way. Then, you can partake in the serious business of enjoying yourself. It would be a lovely day to visit an elderly relative or put your time and energy into home improvements.

## Monday 17th

There may be a lot of good cheer in your life connected to your home and family, or perhaps you're setting off on a journey into your past. Nothing is clear or set in stone now, so assume nothing and keep your options open. Celebrate your wins and be patient with loved ones.

## Tuesday 18th

The more you put into life, the more you get back in return. It may be an age-old saying but there's a lot of truth in it. It's a timely reminder to make the most of what you have and delight in the joys of life. Nothing is permanent so cherish every moment.

## Wednesday 19th

This isn't the time to sit and do nothing. Instead, make the most of some positive feel-good astrology. You might be proud of a child, meet someone irresistible, gain kudos for an artistic achievement or get tickets for a much-desired form of entertainment. Live your life fully.

## Thursday 20th

Eclipses often bring what's hidden to light. Today's solar eclipse is a time to dig deeper into your life. What do you have to let go of or give up before you can enjoy yourself fully? Ask yourself the right questions and answer them honestly.

## Friday 21st

Communication planet Mercury turns retrograde today in your work and health zone. Watch out for the unexpected and take the pace slow. Also, Mercury's your partner planet. Enjoy yourself in a relationship but don't feel that you have to make a major commitment or decision just yet.

## Saturday 22nd

Whatever's taking place behind closed doors, do more of what you love, whether you feel creative or you're chasing after romance. If you're a parent, this could be a definitive time when you're questioning your parenting skills, or perhaps a child requires some extra motivation.

## Sunday 23rd

Your love life is under the cosmic spotlight. New love could begin in dramatic fashion or come about synchronistically. This may open you up to your feelings and emotions that you haven't experienced for some time in a way that's wonderful but potentially unsettling too.

## Monday 24th

Mercury retrograde can slow you down but it's a positive three week period for exploration, fact-finding and research. Go back to someone you met previously, whether this concerns a work or a health matter. Catch up with old contacts. Someone may step in today to help you out financially.

## Tuesday 25th

If a job recently came to an end, be persistent in trying to find alternative employment. Turn to someone older and wiser for sage advice. You may have to dig deep to stay on track with your responsibilities, both at work and home. Knuckle down and get on with the job at hand.

## Wednesday 26th

If you're typical of your star sign, you have an extravagant nature and you're more of a spender than a saver. There may be a wake-up call today or a reality check if you've recently taken your eye off the ball financially. Team up with someone you trust and come up with a plan.

## Thursday 27th

If you're seeking inspiration, it's an ideal day to line up some long-term goals. It's easy to get caught up in the mundane and everyday, but don't lose sight of your dreams. Take one small step towards a future goal, whether that's signing up for a course or booking a trip away.

## Friday 28th

You may have to pull some strings if you're to get time off work today but that might be what needs to happen. Adventure's calling and you won't want to miss out. If you're seeking something more from life, engage actively with politics or social issues to find a bigger purpose.

## Saturday 29th

A lot depends on what's happening at your place of work. You may be asked to help unexpectedly and it's up to you to decide what's right. If money is key to your future progress, put earnings first. If there's someone you don't want to let down, be there for them.

## Sunday 30th

If someone in your family life is struggling because they're unemployed, make the time to talk things through with them and come up with ideas. It's easy to slip into impossibility when the going gets tough. You could be the one to remind them of what opportunities are available.

# MAY

·················

## Monday 1st

There's an inner process taking place now, potentially transforming who you are. Look after yourself on all levels and endeavour to be your best self. There's no rush. Learn to trust in life and listen out for any synchronicities. Learn from the challenges and celebrate the wins.

## Tuesday 2nd

There could be a revelation if you're catching up with an old friend today. Some news or information that you hear could rock your world. The wheel of fortune continues to turn as you ride the highs and lows of life. Sometimes, the more intense something is, the deeper the chance to learn.

## Wednesday 3rd

If you're a typical Sagittarius, you have something of a reputation for being tactless. You tend to leap in without thinking and that's why you can be disarmingly honest at times. Take care today what you reveal to one of your friends as this could act as a trigger.

## Thursday 4th

Love planet Venus remains light-footed in Gemini and your relationship zone. This feels romantic, wistful and yearning and you may be longing for love. If a new relationship is beginning, ensure you take the pace slow and be wary of seduction or promises that can't be kept.

## Friday 5th

Today's lunar eclipse highlights your work and health, as well as your subconscious and inner motivations. This eclipse is about reassessing your life and looking at what works for you and what doesn't. Listen carefully and don't ignore your inner voice if you know something is out.

## Saturday 6th

Wherever you're flagging or feeling low, the recent eclipse may highlight where change is needed. There's a possibility that one form of work is coming to an end. If so, try and be accepting of what's happening. Know that this period is about clearing out so you can start afresh.

## Sunday 7th

Put your needs first today and steer clear of anyone who's giving off negative vibes. It's not going help you to complain about current events, whether there's a health issue or a job loss to contend with. Pull together as a family and consider how to pool your resources and help one another.

## Monday 8th

Challenging emotions could surface but resist the urge to push them down. Ignoring what's happening will only make things worse. Admittedly, you may want to wait until after work before having a good cry with a confidante. Once you've done so, you're likely to feel much lighter.

## Tuesday 9th

When it comes to your work or health, the theme is change.
If you know that doing the same thing time and again isn't
working, look at what you can do differently. You could make a
radical move in one of these areas. Prioritise your wellbeing.

## Wednesday 10th

Don't get caught up in an argument about money or earnings
as it's not going to help. You could end up being the scapegoat
with other people blaming you for what's wrong. Do what's
right for you and ignore the naysayers. What you want to
spend your money on is your choice.

## Thursday 11th

Your inner pessimist could take hold first thing. If so, take
some deep breaths. Rather than worry about what someone
else thinks of you, channel your emotions into a positive
pursuit. Be around people who lift your spirits, write a
gratitude list and aim for a more balanced life outlook.

## Friday 12th

As a Sagittarius, you don't usually have a gloomy nature.
However, you could get pulled into the doldrums now,
especially if you're worrying about your work, a parent or
a family issue. It's important to be realistic about what's
happening but don't let your mind spiral out of control.

## Saturday 13th

If anything's been causing you sleepless nights, now's the
time to reach out and find the help and support you need.
It's invariably true that a problem shared is a problem halved,
however trite it may sound. Turn to your loved ones or find a
friend and seek reassurance.

## Sunday 14th

Take a rain check on your social plans today and line up some much-needed 'me time' instead. You may have discovered a project or hobby that you're passionate about and you want to devote yourself to it. Alternatively, you might enjoy lounging around and doing very little.

## Monday 15th

Communication planet Mercury is now direct. This is great for chasing up news about a work or health matter. Get in the know and find out the facts. This is what Mercury turning direct can be useful for, whether you're awaiting a health diagnosis or applying for a job.

## Tuesday 16th

Big planet Jupiter is on the move today. This is good news if you're looking for a job or you want to make your lifestyle work better for you. Put new habits in place that boost your wellbeing. This is about quality of life and ensuring that you're fit and healthy in mind, body and soul.

## Wednesday 17th

Your ruling planet Jupiter is linked to optimism. Therefore, the more positive you are, the more in sync you are with life. Aim to be less cynical. Try and believe that good things will happen and come your way. Have faith and trust in life. Start a new role as a volunteer.

## Thursday 18th

Get tough on yourself in a good way. Consider your commute, your stress levels or what you do for a living. If you're over-worked or under-worked, change things around. You might be exposing wrong-doings, or be keen to bring new morals and values into the workplace or your community.

## Friday 19th

Today's new moon in Taurus promises new beginnings at work or concerning your health. Use the new moon to set your intentions around these areas or apply for a job. It's a great date to start a fitness plan or consider your diet and health. Prioritise your wellbeing.

## Saturday 20th

Action planet Mars enters fire sign Leo as well as your travel and study zone today, which is wonderful for you. Wherever you find Mars, this is where you find passion and desire. Look out for a new opportunity that lands in your lap this weekend. If it does, grab it with both hands.

## Sunday 21st

You may decide not to go on holiday or to cancel your plans for a study course. This might be because you've met someone new or recent events could have helped you see that you don't want to do things alone. Whatever transpires, trust in life.

## Monday 22nd

This could be a time of dramatic events, or perhaps your beliefs and principles are being challenged. You might be taking a stand for what you believe in or want to expose any corruption or wrong-doings. This could be the trigger that sets you on a new path.

## Tuesday 23rd

If you're typical of your star sign, you don't give up easily when there's something you want in life. What takes place now could see you fighting for your rights or going all out to get a place on a course or workshop. If you're a teacher, you may be on a mission.

## Wednesday 24th

If something's not worked out recently, this could be spurring you on to bigger and better things. You're an adventurer at heart and you may be rediscovering the travel bug. If you're keen to go on a sabbatical or spend the summer abroad, you're in tune with your stars.

## Thursday 25th

Expand your experience of life in any direction you choose. Whether you're getting into politics, setting out as a teacher or you're on a spiritual path, don't settle for less than you deserve. This is about your happiness, your emotional fulfilment and finding a new life purpose.

## Friday 26th

You could find an unlikely ally at your place of work. Talk to a colleague you don't know very well and you could be delighted with their take on life. Be open-minded and willing to hear what other people have to say. Ask for help today and your wish could be granted.

## Saturday 27th

Keep your eyes firmly fixed on a long-term goal. When you're willing to take a risk, have a big vision and believe in what you're doing, anything's possible. Life could throw you a curveball and remind you that life is short. If you're seeking your true vocation, take one small step today.

## Sunday 28th

You may be saying goodbye to someone you care about today, or perhaps you know it's time to move away from a challenging situation that's been holding you back. There could be some sadness involved but that's often the way when the future takes precedence over the past.

## Monday 29th

If you know you're not on the right path, commit to explore new avenues today. Sometimes, that's all it takes to set you off in the right direction. You might not know exactly where you're heading or why. What matters is you believe there's something more ahead.

## Tuesday 30th

Be around other people today and this will benefit you in different ways. Firstly, you're an extrovert at heart and at your best when you have a wide social circle and friends from different cultures and backgrounds. Secondly, you could hear about a project that's right up your street.

## Wednesday 31st

If you want to help out a friend, offer them time rather than money today. You may not see eye to eye with someone, but don't make a big thing of it. Notice if you're feeling envious or unloved. Your emotional state is likely being triggered.

# JUNE
. . . . . . . . . . . . . . . . . .

### Thursday 1st
You could feel as if you're out of control today. You may want to take steps towards a future goal, but perhaps you're feeling tired or doubting your progress. You could throw everything at a project including the kitchen sink, but try and conserve your energy instead.

### Friday 2nd
Pace yourself as the working week comes to a close. You might prefer to be under the duvet and take care of yourself rather than deal with meetings and tricky customers. This evening, ensure comfort is your main priority. Ask your other half to cook for you or take care of you.

### Saturday 3rd
This weekend's full moon is potent for you as it falls in your star sign. Whatever your current relationship situation, this promises drama and excitement or, at least, important lessons and learning around love and partnership. Consider where you may need to take back your power.

### Sunday 4th
Think about how you use technology today. It would be a great time to start an internet campaign or network online. As love is under the cosmic spotlight, you could consider joining a dating site. Reassess your one-to-ones so they are working for you and not against you.

## Monday 5th

The planet of connection Venus enters the part of your horoscope where you find meaning in life. The more you broaden your horizons, the more fulfilled you feel. This will help you remain curious about life and all that's on offer now and over the next few months. Keep exploring what's new.

## Tuesday 6th

It may be a case of back to the drawing board today if things didn't work out towards the end of last week. Have another go at presenting your ideas or talking to a client. You have a greater chance of success now. Get serious, think about the money involved and act accordingly.

## Wednesday 7th

You might be up against opposition today, or perhaps you're comparing yourself to other peoples' achievements. Either way, take a step back and use your logical brain to decide what comes next rather than leap in all guns blazing. As a Sagittarius, it's worth remembering that less is more.

## Thursday 8th

Technology could prove tricky today so don't rely on it too heavily. If you use social media for your career or your business, make sure you use different websites rather than put all your eggs in one basket. You can get to know someone better during a lunchtime date or meeting.

## Friday 9th

If you can work from home today, that would be preferable. You're probably slowing down and getting ready for the weekend. If you haven't seen much of your family or loved ones recently, make them your priority over the next few days. Try not to let fear or scarcity kick in.

## Saturday 10th

Do what's right for you emotionally. If that means saying no to visiting your partner's family, be firm. There's a possibility that you're going to get pulled in too many different directions and lose sight of your anchor or what grounds you. Deal with your work and money issues head-on.

## Sunday 11th

There's some big astrology taking place and a money worry could be back to haunt you. Make one last effort to rid yourself of a financial or emotional tie. Give yourself a goal to be free by the end of the year. If you need support, talk to someone.

## Monday 12th

It's a lively start to the week and, hopefully, you're feeling rested after the weekend. The more fun you have today, the more you'll get done. If you're working towards a long-term project or you have your eye on your future goals, be bold and take a well-calculated risk.

## Tuesday 13th

Engage with your one-to-ones and know that there's a theme of secrets. You may be the one hiding your inner desires, or perhaps you discover that someone else hasn't revealed the whole truth. Dig deep to find out what's happening as this could affect you financially.

## Wednesday 14th

You may be covering for a colleague who's on holiday this week, or perhaps you're living vicariously through social media and holiday snaps from your friends. Your turn will come. For now, know that it's through your work that you may find abundance and emotional fulfilment.

## Thursday 15th

It's not easy when duty or responsibilities hold you back and stop you from living the life you choose. Yet, the reality could be that you have to be there for other people, or perhaps your living situation has to change before you can be free to go wherever you want.

## Friday 16th

Today would be an excellent date for a meeting or interview. Line up a conversation that can move things forward and fast. You can think on your feet now, make a snap decision and leap into a spontaneous conversation. Don't avoid the serious issues and deal with them head-on.

## Saturday 17th

There could be an important shift in your home or family life this weekend, perhaps involving a parent or the place you grew up. You may choose to do things differently to prioritise your children or grandchildren, or you may change things around to benefit your emotional wellbeing.

## Sunday 18th

Today's new moon falls in Gemini, your opposite star sign. This highlights your one-to-one relationships, both personal and professional. You're wise to get on the right side of people of influence over the next couple of weeks and notice who can help you make swift progress.

## Monday 19th

Not everyone may approve of what you're committing to, but don't let that stop you. This could be a significant period when you're making a decision that affects not only your daily routine but your family as well. Prioritise your good health or step in to ensure a parent's good health.

## Tuesday 20th

You may be fearful of letting go today, whether this is linked to money or your past. You might have to make a bold move linked to family money or taking care of your loved ones. A new chapter is beginning and you may need to prioritise these.

## Wednesday 21st

Do you believe you're good with money or do you hand your finances over to other people? Does money arouse strong emotions in you, such as guilt, envy, fear? This would be an ideal time to delve deeper into the world of money. Consider your values and what money means to you.

## Thursday 22nd

Get other people on board if you decide you want to invest in your education or you're saving up for a holiday. The more support you have in your life, the better. Gather the troops and consider all your options. A summer of adventure beckons as long as you make some decisive moves fast.

## Friday 23rd

You may receive a bonus or investment now or, perhaps an inheritance or gift of money comes your way. Certainly, it's a good time to team up with other people to attract abundance into your life. When you find the right financial partnership, your money could increase.

## Saturday 24th

It may be the weekend but the moon is lighting up your career and vocation zone. You may choose to work today, especially if the money's good, or perhaps you're thinking about building a part-time business or setting up a volunteering group close to where you live.

## Sunday 25th

If you're in a relationship or married, this isn't the time to make assumptions or make a major decision around love. This might relate to your family as well. You could find that your emotions are closely attuned to what's happening in the lives of the ones you love.

## Monday 26th

Tempers could flare at the start of the week. This isn't the best time to get involved in an argument, especially regarding your work or a health or medical issue. Instead, take a step back and prioritise your needs. You might be disappointed about a holiday situation but don't give up on your plans.

## Tuesday 27th

There may be someone in your family who's dealing with a financial issue and you want to do your bit to help. When it comes to money, take a cautious approach and aim to save more and spend less. It's an excellent date to find the right financial adviser to meet your needs.

## Wednesday 28th

It's a promising date to find out what's going on behind the scenes. Choose your words carefully and someone close could open up about what's happening in their life. Tackle a taboo issue and do so compassionately and sensitively. Give strong support to a loved one.

## Thursday 29th

Consider carefully whether you're ready to take on more responsibility. Create firm boundaries in your life and put new rules in place that benefit you and your family. Think about your security and look at ways of creating firm foundations for yourself and the ones you love.

## Friday 30th

You might be enjoying jovial connections with loved ones or people from your past this weekend. There could be a lot of good cheer in your life connected to home and family. Or, perhaps you're setting off on a journey delving deep into your past, whether literal or metaphorical.

# JULY
..................

## Saturday 1st

You could be jumping for joy today. You might hear good news about a health issue or a job. Alternatively, your partner is the one who's doing well and gives you both reasons to celebrate. If you can help today, do what you can to put a smile on someone's face.

## Sunday 2nd

Your plans could change suddenly. You may be disappointed when a friend pulls out of a big event. Show willingness and be flexible and know that the situation isn't final. Sometimes, life has a way of pointing you in the right direction even if it doesn't feel like it at the time.

## Monday 3rd

All kinds of money matters and financial transactions are under the cosmic spotlight today. Something could come to light wherever another person's input or decision affects your own. This can indicate your money ties or the places and people who have control over your assets.

## Tuesday 4th

Look out for a cash conflict or opposing needs or wants regarding money and material matters. A third party may be involved, whether this is someone trying to get their hands on your money, or someone who's willing to help you out financially. Cut through to the heart of the matter.

## Wednesday 5th

Be careful you're not too stuck in your ways today and be willing to experiment. There's a fine line between sticking to a tried and tested route and getting bored of what you're doing. Open your eyes to new ideas and technologies as this could help strengthen your position.

## Thursday 6th

When it comes to foreign connections, don't rely solely on technology. Double-check that a text or email has reached its destination. Choose your confidantes carefully now and steer clear of a person who could try to talk you out of your exciting plans regarding travel or study.

## Friday 7th

It would be a good day to consult an accountant to ensure that your money is invested well. If you're running short of cash, consider all your options and lean on family or someone from your past for help or support. A part-time job or overtime could be a quick-fix solution.

## Saturday 8th

You might want to escape from reality today and switch off completely. It would be a good day to dive under the duvet with a good book or binge-watch your favourite TV programme. What's not wise is to give in to boredom. Line up a fun social event this evening.

## Sunday 9th

Crack on with a money-making venture and ensure that your money is safe and secure. Take a well-calculated risk, especially around a property matter or regarding your home and family. Have faith that things will work out. Dig deep to make the right money moves.

## Monday 10th

Ambitious Mars enters your career and vocation zone today. This is the start of a potentially successful couple of months when you'll be required to work hard. As a Sagittarius, you often have a big vision for your life, but Mars in Virgo is about drawing up the business plan.

## Tuesday 11th

If you're a typical Sagittarius, you need things in life to look forward to and you're always considering the bigger picture. You're the explorer and philosopher of the zodiac and this is a week when you'll be stimulated by the possibility of holidays, trips and learning.

## Wednesday 12th

If an income stream recently came to an end or the promise of money didn't materialise, consider your next options. An online business is one possibility, or perhaps a chance to diversify from your usual job or career. Get creative and explore new possibilities via the internet.

## Thursday 13th

There could be a clash of opinions today and you may want to limit your communications. When you ask for everybody's viewpoint, you invariably get different answers. Rather than reach out to a host of people to decide what's right for you, ask the person who knows you best.

## Friday 14th

Take note of a conversation that happens today or a new opportunity that arises. This could be about work and money, or alternatively your health and wellbeing. A snap decision might prove lucrative or beneficial. It's a good day to get on the right side of a possible business partner.

## Saturday 15th

Aim to be more business-oriented moving forward. If you're typical of your star sign, you trust in life and make a good entrepreneur. What you're not always good at is the boring or mundane side of work. Outsource what you don't like doing and ensure you have a strong team around you.

## Sunday 16th

This is a significant time of year for all kinds of partnership. When you get the right people on your side, you make quicker progress. Whether you're looking for a cleaner, an accountant, or a PA, invest in people whose expertise and abilities can save you time and money in the long run.

## Monday 17th

Today's new moon lights up your joint finance zone. There may be a significant shift around money now, or perhaps you hear news or information about a job or contract that arises unexpectedly. It's a good date to act fast and be spontaneous. Set up a new savings plan.

## Tuesday 18th

You could feel stirred up or frustrated around a financial issue. Take care that you don't lash out. It might be time to resolve one money matter permanently and fight for what's yours. However, do this in a way that's just and fair and consider your motivations carefully before leaping in.

## Wednesday 19th

Get on the phone or send an email today and move one of your big dreams forward. It's an excellent date to find out more about an educational course or study holiday that's perfect for you. Take even one small step towards a future goal and your excitement levels will rise.

## Thursday 20th

Today's tricky astrology could flag up an issue at work or home. Something may come to an end, or perhaps you're feeling angry about an unfair situation. Even so, choose your battles carefully. Don't waste your energy and discern which issues to pick up on and which to drop.

## Friday 21st

You might have a tough choice to make, especially if you feel pulled between the future and the past. Where there's strong energy in your horoscope is your career zone. It might be hard to disappoint someone in your family, but the stars are aligned to boost your status and reputation.

## Saturday 22nd

You're entering into a period of unknowing, exploration and experimentation. Keep your options open and question what you read or hear. Don't take anything at face value and don't worry if you haven't got all the answers or the cash. When the plan is right, the rest will materialise.

## Sunday 23rd

Venus turns retrograde today and will be in retreat for the next six weeks. This is a reflective phase when you may need time alone to think things through. If you want to change external events, start by working on your inner self. Go somewhere different to speed up the change.

## Monday 24th

Fire sign Leo rules travel and study in your horoscope and the bigger picture. This is where you feel at home if you're a typical Sagittarius. You're the explorer and philosopher of the zodiac and this is a great week for embracing holidays, study and learning. Let the Sun in Leo lead the way.

## Tuesday 25th

Keep talking if you're trying to organise a big event for a group of your friends. It might feel like you're herding cats, but stay willing and be open to whatever comes your way. A school or college reunion would be a perfect way to embrace the Venus retrograde phase.

## Wednesday 26th

You're in your element when planets move through fire signs. There's likely to be a shift in pace now. You may want to spend less time focused on money and more time being social and planning what next. Take a step back so you can move forward with confidence.

## Thursday 27th

The Venus retrograde phase could bring an old lover back into your life, someone you met abroad or while you were studying. This might be a time of rich emotion and precious memories. When you move beyond your comfort zone and say yes to life, this is where fulfilment lies.

## Friday 28th

If you've felt overwhelmed recently, this week's astrology gives you a burst of energy and a positive can-do attitude. What's calling you is a holiday or a change of scene. Step out of the same-old routine and shift things around. Be a sun-seeker as this may inspire new ideas.

## Saturday 29th

If a new relationship is beginning, take the pace slow and be wary of seduction or promises that can't be kept. You could be led astray in affairs of the heart now, so keep your wits about you. If you have an emotional blind spot around a certain individual, keep your eyes wide open.

## Sunday 30th

Communication planet Mercury is in your career zone. You could be juggling a lot of different projects or tasks. What Mercury in Virgo is good for is being systematic and organised. Spend time today getting ready for the week ahead. You need to learn to work smart, not hard.

## Monday 31st

You might be teaching others this week or learning something new. This has a lot to do with the coming full moon that cuts across the travel and study zones of your horoscope. The focus is on your education, gaining knowledge and sharing your skills and talents with others.

# AUGUST

· · · · · · · · · · · · · · · · · ·

## Tuesday 1st

Full moons often coincide with completion or culmination in life. The light of the moon is at its brightest and you can see things with clarity. This is a great time to make a decision about travel, study, religion, the law, publishing or publicity, all Sagittarius themes.

## Wednesday 2nd

Work or your everyday routine could be holding you back. You might have to cover for someone who's away on holiday at work. Alternatively, you may want to change your routine so you can do something that appeals to the adventurous side of your nature. Be courageous.

## Thursday 3rd

You may be frustrated if someone's not taking you seriously now. This might be someone at work or an older member of your family. Be aware, however, that miscommunications are likely. Therefore, it's worth double-checking what someone means before leaping in to defend yourself.

## Friday 4th

You may have one foot in the past and one foot in the future now. As much as you might want to push ahead and be ambitious, you could be emotionally attached to what other people think of you. Either that, or old beliefs are kicking in. If so, try your best to banish them from your mind.

## Saturday 5th

There are times when you're wise to leap into life and not spend too much time navel-gazing or examining your emotional state. This weekend is ideal for doing more of what you love so put any unsettling emotions to one side. Being around children could be the perfect antidote.

## Sunday 6th

Embrace life fully and set off on a grand adventure. If you're travelling today, you're in tune with your stars. If you're on a workshop exploring your spirituality or your personal transformation, perfect. It's a lovely time to expand your experience of life.

## Monday 7th

You may be more aware than most that luck is an attitude. Luck doesn't necessarily find you if you're sitting doing nothing. Instead, you have to make your luck by being willing to take risks and have a strong sense of self-belief. Get your team on your side today and aim to win.

## Tuesday 8th

You could have a positive influence on your workplace now. This might be because you're interested in people and want to ensure your colleagues get their rights met, or perhaps you're bringing your morals and ethics into the workplace. Either way, it's a winning combination.

## Wednesday 9th

If you're typical of your star sign, you're a free spirit at heart. This can mean you enjoy being in an unconventional relationship where you still have your freedom or independence. Sometimes, this works in your favour and sometimes it doesn't. Be ready for the unexpected today.

## Thursday 10th

It's an excellent day to look ahead, especially when it comes to your career, your vocation and future path. If you're looking for work or you're seeking a promotion, be proactive. This could be the day you get your lucky break and hear the news you've been waiting for.

## Friday 11th

You could choose to tell a little white lie today so that you don't hurt someone else's feelings. Your partner may not understand why you're prioritising your projects over your relationship, or perhaps you don't want to upset someone in your family unnecessarily. Do whatever feels right.

## Saturday 12th

Turn your attention to family finances and start to think about your future security. You may be helping someone close get their foot on the property ladder, or perhaps you're the one who's seeking firmer foundations in your life. There's a serious vibe to your stars so pay attention.

## Sunday 13th

Today's Sun-Venus conjunction is significant for you. This could be the right time to reach out to someone in a position of influence who can help you. This may be a teacher or guru or someone with foreign connections. You may hear from a lover, present or past, who lives abroad.

## Monday 14th

You could let money stop you from doing what you want, or you could decide to say yes to your dreams and trust that the money will come. It's a fine line to walk and you need to tread carefully. There could be a chance, however, to let go of a limiting belief once and for all.

## Tuesday 15th

Your infectious enthusiasm and joy of life could rub off on other people and you end up having a fun day at work. Laughter is definitely the best medicine. The more in tune you are with your adventurous spirit, the healthier you are in mind, body and soul.

## Wednesday 16th

You could experience an inner revolution today. Flex your rebellious muscle and refuse to be held back by the conventions of society. As a Sagittarius, you're at your best when walking your path and believing that anything's possible.

## Thursday 17th

It's a good time to initiate something new around travel or study, even if it means a change to your original plans. Let boredom be your trigger and shake free of a situation that's holding you back. There are always solutions to problems, especially when you start asking around.

## Friday 18th

You may be in the public eye today or over the weekend. Perhaps you're presenting or stepping into a teaching role. You may be leading an important meeting or be on the board of governors at a local school. Play your part within society and stand up for what you believe in.

## Saturday 19th

If there's someone in your life who knows how to put a guilt trip upon you, it's probably wise to avoid them today. This could be a parent or someone from your past. Arrange a social event with your friends or be proactive within a group, club or society of which you're a member.

## Sunday 20th

Line up a life-enhancing activity today, ideally with a group of friends. Higher education often plays a key role within your life and you rarely stop learning. Any environment that offers harmony, supportive relationships and spiritual development is the place to be.

## Monday 21st

Be careful of giving too much now and over the next few days. If you're a typical Sagittarius, you often have a wide social circle and you get involved in community ventures. As you're entering into a busy phase, it's important not to hit burnout. Fan the flames that boost your spirit.

## Tuesday 22nd

You might be feeling sentimental about the past today or be emotional about what's going on in the world or your personal life. Try not to let the past hold you back from taking the next big step. Use your emotions to fuel your ambition.

## Wednesday 23rd

The Sun's move into Virgo today is about your career and vocation, your status and reputation. There's no point in holding back now. Instead, go all out to make your name and get yourself noticed. Give yourself the next three weeks to line up a new job, role or project.

## Thursday 24th

Communication planet Mercury is now retrograde in your career zone. This is an indication to keep your eye on the prize, prioritise your career and vocation but not to make any major decisions. It's an excellent period to chase up old contacts.

## Friday 25th

You may be considering a new career path, one that's more in sync with who you are. When you engage in personal transformation work, this can reveal new layers to your personality. The stronger your self-belief, the more you value yourself and can be paid what you deserve.

## Saturday 26th

Decide what's not working out and where or how you can cut costs today. This may be the time to stop a drain on your finances, for example. Get real about money and make some firm commitments. Even one small change to your habits can make a big difference.

## Sunday 27th

Action planet Mars enters your friendship and group zone today. You may become more involved with a club or society over the next couple of months. Passion is potentially on the cards and love and friendship are linked. Don't give up the day job but do seek inspiration elsewhere.

## Monday 28th

An early start today could benefit you, especially if you've got mundane chores or administration to deal with. Try not to procrastinate and get the most boring jobs out of the way first. As the day goes on, it becomes more social and you could have a blast with a new set of friends.

## Tuesday 29th

Ideally, you won't be working 9-5 now or you could feel trapped in your current situation. This week's astrology is encouraging you to embrace freedom or at least be flexible with your time so you can do what you want when you want and have more choice in your routine.

## Wednesday 30th

Full moons are often times of heightened emotion. Make sure you tap into your feelings now and don't be afraid of releasing them. If someone in your past taught you not to express yourself fully and that crying was weak, actively surrender to your feelings and break down the dam.

## Thursday 31st

Today's full moon cuts across the foundations of your horoscope. This could coincide with a major achievement or acknowledgement. Alternatively, it could bring a sea-change to family life. Someone may be moving on or you're saying goodbye to a home or a chapter in your life.

# SEPTEMBER

### Friday 1st

You may be extra sensitive today. It could be a challenge not to overreact to a negative comment or not to burst into tears when a memory pops up. Lunchtime onwards could be less emotional, especially when you engage actively with life. Turn any anger into passion.

### Saturday 2nd

You could be on the verge of a significant turning point in your life when you're ready to put play before work and pleasure before duty. Catching up with a friend who lives abroad could be the trigger that sets you free. Closer to home, meet up with your friends.

### Sunday 3rd

An issue around money or low self-esteem isn't going to disappear overnight. However, it's important that you don't let either of these issues hold you back. Come 2024, you're going to be starting with a clean slate and this could include an easier year ahead financially.

### Monday 4th

You could experience less pressure from today regarding your work or your health. Take your foot off the brake and celebrate a job well done. You may be taking the bold step to leave a job behind to pursue a life-long dream. Embrace new ideas and new experiences in your life.

## Tuesday 5th

It's worth getting up early if you want to send out a lot of emails or do some research online. Your current astrology favours freelance work or a temporary contract. This evening, make time for love, especially if you've been too busy of late to spend quality time with your other half.

## Wednesday 6th

One conversation could make a huge difference today. If you've been thinking about applying for a new role or job or you want to gain the support of someone in a position of influence, make it happen. Someone you know through a previous career could get back in touch.

## Thursday 7th

If there are any issues within a close relationship, you may be more aware of them at the moment. Firstly, try and identify what the problem might be, whether it's an emotional mismatch or one of you has extra responsibilities that can't be relinquished. Secondly, engage with one another.

## Friday 8th

Today's astrology is packed full of good fortune. You might land a new job, hear about an opportunity to work abroad or be asked to teach, present or share your experiences. This is not the time to play small. Stretch your comfort zone and say yes to a new opportunity.

## Saturday 9th

This is a powerful time for manifestation. One of the blessings that your ruling planet Jupiter bestows upon you is the ability to remain optimistic and be philosophical about life, even when times are tough. Look out for the person who steps up and offers you a gift or compliment.

## Sunday 10th

You may be feeling more emotionally intense today. You could be unusually contrary or experience some conflict or opposition that affects your mood. Try not to let negativity bring you down and don't take on other people's problems. Create a protective light or bubble around you.

## Monday 11th

Love has a foreign theme, whether you're on holiday or you're getting together with someone you met on a course or place of study. If you're in a relationship or married, arrange something special with your other half and try something new together. Turn your gaze towards the future.

## Tuesday 12th

You could experience changeable emotions today and your mood may be more erratic than usual. You could blag a sickie at work or act spontaneously to change around your schedule to suit you. Any issues at work could take a turn for the better come the end of the week.

## Wednesday 13th

Earth sign energy doesn't always fit easily with your lively fire sign nature. Yet, if you want to get ahead and make things happen, you can learn a lot from the slower-moving, predictable element. Take one step at a time, day in day out, and before you know it, you've covered a lot of ground.

## Thursday 14th

Get work and money matters in order this week. Manage your time, be efficient and organised. This is the way to use the earth element to its utmost potential. There's a link to the past as the wheel of karma turns. You could discover a secret or wrongdoing.

## Friday 15th

Listen out for a new career or vocational opportunity on today's new moon. Set your intentions for the year ahead or even further down the line and draw up a 5 or 10-year plan. This would be an excellent date to launch a new project or send off a job application.

## Saturday 16th

This is a time when you have to speak up, however radical or controversial your thoughts. You can't be happy with yourself if you don't say what you're thinking, especially if this is about world events and the society we live in. Your world might also be your place of work.

## Sunday 17th

Take your foot off the work pedal and have fun. This is particularly important if you've been busy recently or you've been busy rethinking and reworking your future steps. It would be an ideal Sunday for a day trip. Go somewhere you've never been before, preferably with the one you love.

## Monday 18th

You may need some time to mull over recent events today. When you have a lot of external change, it can take time for your inner equilibrium to catch up. There's a possibility that you won't get much done in the daytime but you may get a creative streak later on.

## Tuesday 19th

You may be more susceptible to confusion or seduction today. Keep your feet on the ground, pay close attention to the facts and discern what's true and what's not. You may need an anchor in life so you don't drift away. Tap into your creative imagination.

## Wednesday 20th

Listen carefully to your intuition first thing and don't discount what you're hearing. It would be easy to get caught up in the hustle and bustle of life or be cut off from your intuition on social media. Your right-brain thinking can be a better guide now than left-brain logic.

## Thursday 21st

It's an excellent day for drawing up new ideas to pay off a debt or massively improve your financial situation. Write things down and pay attention to the details. When you state your intentions clearly, you have a better chance of manifesting them. Sign or seal a contract.

## Friday 22nd

Notice where in life you're feeling out of sorts or you don't fit in. Instead of allowing this to unsettle you, make a conscious decision to stand your ground and put your needs first. Deal with what's real today rather than lose yourself in a fantasy world. Do the sums, balance the books.

## Saturday 23rd

The Sun's move into Libra today is a reminder to be out in the world and to balance play and work. However, it's not only about socialising and friends. This is about teamwork and creating joint ventures that will help you continue what you've been working on over the last few weeks.

## Sunday 24th

Put firm boundaries in place around money. Whether this means spending sensibly depends on your current situation. Either way, it's around your money and your finances where you're wise to be cautious. When in doubt, act conservatively.

## Monday 25th

Your positive attitude and natural generosity could come back to reward you now. This may be in the shape of good news, a new qualification or a favour that's returned. Be proud of yourself for your achievements but, more importantly, be proud of yourself for the person you've become.

## Tuesday 26th

Technology could let you down today, especially if you're trying to communicate online with someone who lives abroad. Have a backup plan and ideally reschedule for another time. You may in your local community by asking other people to share their ideas.

## Wednesday 27th

Supporting a member of your family could seem like a burden or responsibility that weighs heavy. However, when you turn grumpiness into gratitude, this can make a huge difference to your life as well as the person you're caring for. Get back in touch with your big-hearted generosity.

## Thursday 28th

Today's full moon cuts across the social axis of your horoscope. This is about your friendships, your social circle, your networks and the people you connect with for fun and inspiration. It's also about your children or your lovers. The light of the full moon may bring clarity.

## Friday 29th

During this full moon phase, it's important to speak up. Whether you join a group or leave a group isn't the point. What's important is to make a decision one way or the other. Say your piece, make a commitment and move on. Money might be the reason for your ultimatum or decision.

## Saturday 30th

You may want to spend the day with your family, but work or responsibilities could get in the way. Try not to flare up angrily if you feel pulled in different directions. Some quick thinking on your part could save the day. Keep a close check on your emails or phone as day turns into night.

# OCTOBER

. . . . . . . . . . . . . . . . . .

## Sunday 1st

Aim for moderation today rather than excess. Decide what that means for you whether it's about your health and fitness or your work and routine. Sometimes, a slow and steady pace really does win the day. Aim to be the tortoise, not the hare and appreciate the small things in life.

## Monday 2nd

You might be in the process of surrendering or letting go of a job, project or work chapter. There could be different reasons why. You may have nothing more to give and nothing new to learn. Alternatively, you may be ready for a new adventure that involves a group or association.

## Tuesday 3rd

Your planet Jupiter is the truth-seeker and truthfulness and authenticity are important qualities for your Sagittarius nature. You may be weighing up the benefits of not revealing the truth today. Think things through carefully before you decide what you want to reveal, especially at work.

## Wednesday 4th

Reach out to other people and hear what they have to say. It's potentially a lovely day for all your close relationships and getting to know new people. When you feel self-confident and attractive to others, this helps you to attract the right kind of person to you.

## Thursday 5th

Communication planet Mercury enters your friendship zone today. Now's the ideal time to hang out with your friends, talk about new adventures and discuss what's next. If you're typical of your star sign, you love to have something new to look forward to. Stay positive without losing hold of reality.

## Friday 6th

Keep the lines of communication open today and see what arises. It could be a change of scene or a new educational course. If you've been thinking about investing in your future, whether for travel or study reasons, it's a positive day to make a commitment and pay accordingly.

## Saturday 7th

An issue that arises around money could turn nasty fast. Think twice before accusing someone and take a step back from an argument that flares up. You may decide to stay late at a party tonight if you want to shake off some difficult emotions.

## Sunday 8th

Get out into the fresh air today and expand your horizons. Sometimes, it's hard to see the wood for the trees when you're up close and personal with whatever's going on. Take a breather and view your situation from a different perspective. Head out on a day trip.

## Monday 9th

There could be conflict around money today if someone close isn't pulling their weight financially. However, it could be more complex and it's not the time to get back with someone from your past. Keep your money safe and avoid angry people. Lean towards the right person at work.

## Tuesday 10th

You may be called back into the family fold today or, perhaps you're finalising building work or recognise that your current accommodation is limiting and you need more space. Think of this as a long-term project, but don't let the more serious side of life stop you from enjoying yourself.

## Wednesday 11th

You're wise to conserve your spending and make some sensible moves and firm plans for the future. This might be to help someone in your family or to improve your living conditions. It's here where you can make the most difference. Be careful what you hook your esteem onto.

## Thursday 12th

Listen out for insights or new information that emerges now and over the next few days. You may be plotting and planning your next steps or be more introverted than usual. Gather your thoughts, don't waste your precious energy and share important knowledge or wisdom with others.

## Friday 13th

It's wise to keep a healthy work/life balance and it may become evident why over the weekend. If you're busy or spending too much time alone, you could become frustrated. Don't turn difficult emotions in on yourself. Instead, learn to express and release your emotions effectively.

## Saturday 14th

Today's solar eclipse highlights your friendship and group zone. A good friend may need you and you could choose to drop everything and step in to help. It's a powerful time to resolve a triangle situation so you can put bad feelings behind you. Aim for peace and harmony.

## Sunday 15th

Your friendships could be turbocharged now, which means there's plenty of passion but potentially anger too. One situation could be full-on as tempers flare. If you're involved with a group that's important to you, expect a tempestuous few days as the solar eclipse kicks in.

## Monday 16th

If someone at work has confided in you, you might want to think hard about revealing the information. This doesn't come easily to you, as there's a side of your personality that's naturally honest. Take a step back so you don't reveal all.

## Tuesday 17th

It's important to keep a healthy balance between your responsibilities and your personal happiness. The moon's move through your star sign often reminds you of this truth. If you want to spend more time looking after yourself and working on your personal goals, go for it.

## Wednesday 18th

You may be experiencing a high degree of emotional and psychological self-awareness. If so, you can expand this experience by signing up for a personal growth workshop or spiritual teaching. Be more self-centred because, by doing so, you get to know yourself on a deeper level.

## Thursday 19th

Sit down with your friends and have a truth-telling session. This won't work with everyone but it could be hugely beneficial to the people in your life you know and trust the most. Find new ways to be supportive of one another, whether emotionally or through acts of kindness.

## Friday 20th

Your stars are psychic or intuitive now. Follow up a hunch and listen out for any synchronicities that lead you to contact a friend. You might even wake up before your alarm goes off as a dream feels important to pass on. This could include a warning linked to money or love.

## Saturday 21st

Money requires reassessment this weekend, how to pay the bills or deal with debt, what money means to you and how to use and invest it wisely. Have those tough conversations either with yourself, a friend or frenemy. Get real about money and make a plan.

## Sunday 22nd

Communication planet Mercury enters the most hidden zone of your horoscope today. This is about self-analysis and listening to your inner voice. Mercury is your partner planet too, so this could flag up a secretive or private theme when it comes to love and romantic liaisons.

## Monday 23rd

The Sun enters Scorpio today. You're not usually someone who keeps secrets but you might be asked to keep a confidence over the next few weeks. You could have your own secrets or personal demons to confront. Listen to your inner voice, be more thoughtful, quiet and still.

## Tuesday 24th

This is often a key period of preparation as you move towards the Sun's entry into your star sign on November 22nd. What would benefit you now? More rest? More study or research? More planning? Do whatever feels right for you and actively encourage a slower pace of life.

## Wednesday 25th

It's worth making an extra effort today to impress a person at work. Make sure you're on time and engage actively with whatever's going on. It's not going to be an easy task, especially when they pick up on small details, but do your best to keep things amicable.

## Thursday 26th

You could be tired or unmotivated first thing. Have a lie-in if you can and then get on with the day. Things are likely to get better quickly, especially when you engage with your sense of fun and tap into your creative skills. The more you express yourself fully, the more energised you become.

## Friday 27th

Make the most of the calm before the storm as this weekend's astrology could prove lively. You have a free run through the cosmos to pursue a love affair or do something special with your children. Prioritise good times, entertainment and enjoy a hobby you're passionate about.

## Saturday 28th

There's a lot of storm and noise going on in the cosmos with a lively lunar eclipse taking place. Prioritise your health and take time out if you're feeling unsettled or anxious. One chapter is coming to an end that began in November 2021.

## Sunday 29th

Your relationships may become less important for a while, or perhaps it's more about recognising that you've been investing too much time and energy in another person. This weekend's astrology is ideal for getting back on track with what you need. Listen carefully to your inner voice.

## Monday 30th

You can quickly grow bored of your everyday routine. Therefore, it's important you find a way to ring the changes and keep things fresh. Rejig your schedule. Later on, talk through any challenges in a close relationship. Put some firm boundaries in place that could benefit you both.

## Tuesday 31st

Your love life and your working life may be linked in some way today. Perhaps, you're thinking about someone you know professionally in a romantic context, or maybe a work colleague is flirting with you. Today's astrology could be super lively and a time when anything goes.

# NOVEMBER
· · · · · · · · · · · · · · · · ·

## Wednesday 1st
Listen to your inner voice and try not to dismiss your
unconscious thoughts. If you become fearful or anxious, your
best strategy is to surrender and slow things right down.
Whatever helps you rest and relax; gardening, cooking, a form
of art, meditation or a soak in the bath.

## Thursday 2nd
Focus on the parts of your life that you can control today
and let go of anything that you can't. Worrying about what
someone thinks of you at work won't help anything. Return to
simple pleasures, practise gratitude and keep a daily journal
to help balance your mood.

## Friday 3rd
You may need to rein in your generous nature now, or at least
slow things down. Let other people take the lead where you
can and turn to expert advice if it seems helpful for you. This
might be the right time to consult a lawyer, career coach or
health professional.

## Saturday 4th
Plans could change suddenly and you may be the one initiating
a last-minute alteration. Keep an open mind and question the
information that comes your way. A message from beyond the
grave could be presented to you or a coincidence that takes
you deep into your past.

## Sunday 5th

You could run far away from home today but you would probably still take any worries with you. Rather than try to escape whatever you're feeling, go deeper into your emotions and allow them to take full rein through self-expression or a creative activity. Explore your inner life fully.

## Monday 6th

Go on a journey of the mind today and see where it leads you. There may be some hidden nuggets of truth or knowledge that you can bring to the surface. If a relationship at work has become passionate or intense, you may need to take a step back.

## Tuesday 7th

A secret could come to light now, especially when you learn to ask the right questions. This might be linked to your ancestry, your family or your childhood home. If you want to access your subconscious, turn to art therapy as a medium. Channel your thoughts and feelings into beauty.

## Wednesday 8th

The planet of connection, Venus, moves into Libra today and this shows you where peace and harmony can be found in your life. Libra rules your friendship zone so turn to those people who know how to help you find calm within and can answer your questions or give advice.

## Thursday 9th

There's only so much soul-searching that you can do. If you're a typical Sagittarius, you prefer moving out of the dark spaces and into the light. You may be more than ready to let go of the past and embrace a bright new future. Give your self-esteem a boost and move on.

## Friday 10th

Once communication planet Mercury enters your star sign today, find out who's on your side and who's not. Communicate well and line up key allies to support whatever you're doing. If you're undergoing a period of change, don't hold on tight. Explore your options and embrace new things.

## Saturday 11th

There's an out-of-control vibe going on this weekend. Anger and strong emotions could erupt and fast. On a personal level, look at what you're not prepared to put up with any longer and be wary about taking a foolish risk. Use your passion constructively but rein in your impatience.

## Sunday 12th

You might be involved with a new initiative that tends to the earth. This could be a gardening group, an allotment committee or being part of a bigger organisation linked to tackling climate change. Dust off your wellies, get out in the countryside and breathe in the smells of nature.

## Monday 13th

Set some new intentions on today's new moon. Tap into your deepest emotions and learn to trust your instincts and your inner knowing. Life may step in to point the way forwards. What's going on behind the scenes is as important as what's visible. Ideally, take the day off work if possible.

## Tuesday 14th

What took place yesterday could be more significant than you realise at present. Something hidden could slowly emerge over the next few days, or perhaps you had a shock yesterday linked to your work or a health issue. Initiate a conversation today to try and find out more.

## Wednesday 15th

An upbeat conversation could help to bring insight and understanding to a close relationship. Be there for a good friend and let them know what's been going on for you. It seems as if you're at a significant turning point. You may sense your confidence slowly returning to you.

## Thursday 16th

The more you value yourself highly and know your self-worth, the more this trickles out into the world and can boost your work and your earnings. You may be on a roll today, whether you gain a client or you get an extra-large tip. Being of service to others could bring rewards, both emotional and financial.

## Friday 17th

Today could be perfect for energy work or exploring your psychic capabilities. Listen to your inner voice and try not to dismiss unconscious thoughts that pop up and demand your attention. This may lead you on a journey back into your past and a truthful heart-to-heart with your family.

## Saturday 18th

Don't be scared of confronting a personal issue head-on today. Get to the heart of the matter and go directly for the challenge. It's time to be fearless, to wrestle your inner demons so you can refresh and recharge your batteries. Alternatively, you could be studying hard for an exam.

## Sunday 19th

Find the people who make you happy today and be with the people in your life you enjoy the most. It's an excellent day for a group get-together or social event. There may be things you want to do in preparation for the week ahead but you're unlikely to get round to them. The social scene is where it's at.

## Monday 20th

Sometimes, the easiest way to let go of fear is to express it. When you talk about a personal issue, it's comforting to know that other people have had a similar experience, too. Step out of your comfort zone and speak about a taboo or hidden secret.

## Tuesday 21st

There may be something that you want your family to know about you before they hear it from someone else. You may be implicated in a scandal or wrongdoing but that doesn't mean you've done anything wrong. At the same time, don't be naive and reveal everything.

## Wednesday 22nd

There are two factors taking place this week that spell big news for you. Hopefully, they may bring celebration, vitality and energy your way. Most importantly, it's the start of your birthday month as the Sun moves into your star sign today. It's time for you to shine and take centre stage.

## Thursday 23rd

The Sun rules vitality and warmth and this could bring a burst of confidence or enthusiasm your way. Turn your attention towards your personal goals and aims and boost your image and profile. Shut a door firmly on the past and resolve to move on into a bright new future.

## Friday 24th

Action planet Mars enters Sagittarius today and this adds drive and courage to your personal toolbox. Mars remains in your star sign until January 4th. You may experience a sense that life's speeding up. This puts the spotlight on your personal goals and ambitions outside of work.

## Saturday 25th

One situation could come to an end that may benefit you in the long run. Take a step back from a relationship if necessary to protect yourself. This could be linked to a family relationship. Put boundaries in place or advise someone close to do the same.

## Sunday 26th

It might be Sunday and traditionally a day of rest, but you probably have other ideas. Mars, the physical planet, is now in your star sign so it's great timing to begin a new fitness or health regime. The stronger you are, the more invincible you're going to feel.

## Monday 27th

Today's full moon is about getting your relationships right.
If you're in a relationship that's not working out, expect a
hidden issue to emerge. In a professional partnership, this is
potentially a competitive or argumentative time. A decision
may be made but in a dramatic fashion.

## Tuesday 28th

Full moons often bring resolution to a situation or shine a
light clearly on what's happening. There's a romantic vibe to
this full moon, although perhaps a sense of getting involved
with someone or something that leads you or them astray.
Either way, it's a pivotal moment.

## Wednesday 29th

Money matters might require you to take a fresh look
today, especially if you're subbing someone close or you're
paying money into a bottomless pit. Try to keep money and
relationships separate as best you can. This may be one of the
messages of the full moon.

## Thursday 30th

Look out for a new opportunity that promises freedom and a
chance to break free from debt or a job that holds you back.
It's an excellent day to take a risk and do things differently.
The internet could be your friend whether you're reading job
advertisements or posting on social media.

# DECEMBER
. . . . . . . . . . . . . . . . .

### Friday 1st
Money is an important topic as communication planet
Mercury enters your money zone. This is a time to be sensible
and cautious with your cash. You may want to get ready for
the festive season but have a clear goal in mind. It's a more
productive phase for saving and earning money than spending
wildly.

### Saturday 2nd
Work out a budget for the month ahead, be clear about your
outgoings and spending costs and try and stick to it. The
communication planet will turn retrograde on the 13th in
your money zone. Therefore, ideally, you want to be financially
prepared for the festive season before then.

### Sunday 3rd
It's a good day to declutter, release and let go. You're clearing
away what's old to allow fresh space and energy in. This could
be on a literal level, a psychological or soul level. If a love
relationship's not working out or you're obsessing over a
friend, take a step back.

### Monday 4th
Love planet Venus enters Scorpio today. This can flag up a
theme of secrets or things that are hidden, emerging. Feelings
may intensify over the next few weeks and some things might
have to be kept secret.

## Tuesday 5th

Whatever decision you make in a close relationship, it's important to stick to it. This will be kinder on everyone's feelings, your own included. Trust and loyalty are the bedrock of any long-term relationship or marriage. Happiness comes when you commit to the one you love.

## Wednesday 6th

As you move forward in life, you may sense that you're leaving someone or something behind. You might feel sentimental about the past or emotional about what you've lost. If so, give yourself permission to surrender to your feelings and dive deep into your memories of the past.

## Thursday 7th

If you want to get together with a group of friends to celebrate the festive season, it might be up to you to organise things. You're the one who seems to have a lot of energy and passion. Put it to good use and join in with a community event or be the life and soul of the party.

## Friday 8th

Listen for good news coming your way regarding work or money, perhaps a bonus. You may want to pay your dues or finalise money matters with another person so you're no longer tied together. It would be a lucky day to buy a raffle ticket.

## Saturday 9th

Whatever you're doing this weekend, make sure it's profound. You could flit through life socialising and chatting but the stars are encouraging you to go deeper. If you're a poet, write poetry. If you're a musician, make music. Tap into your creative and spiritual source.

## Sunday 10th

There are some days when you feel happy for no particular reason and this could be one of them. The giving side of your nature could bring happiness to yourself and others. You might be at a charity event or be on a spiritual healing retreat with your best group of friends.

## Monday 11th

The dark side of the moon is traditionally a time to rest and be quiet, to gather your energy ready for the new moon phase which begins tomorrow. If you're extending a weekend away, you're in tune with your stars. This evening is perfect for an intimate date or a one-to-one encounter.

## Tuesday 12th

A new moon in Sagittarius today is excellent for starting a new initiative, turning a page and generally being optimistic about what's next in your life. Move towards gratitude this week with the new moon in your star sign. Look for the positives in life rather than focus on the negatives.

## Wednesday 13th

This is a great time to look ahead and make plans, not only for next month but for 2024 as well. Make a vision board, draw up a list of personal goals and fire those Sagittarius' arrows high into the sky. When you have events to look forward to, it feeds your adventurous spirit.

## Thursday 14th

Cash matters are under the cosmic spotlight. When Mercury is retrograde in your money zone, you know that lessons about money are on the way. You could experience a change of mind or a change of heart. If money is an issue with a partner, this could cause some dissatisfaction.

## Friday 15th

Be aware that the financial picture will change again over the next few weeks, so don't expect to find answers or solutions to money matters straightaway. The message that's coming across loud and clear is to take charge of your affairs rather than leave everything up to other people.

## Saturday 16th

Line up a social event and make sure that you're at the heart of your community over the weekend. Get involved with a school fair, help out at a festive stall on the market and generally enjoy yourself. Catch up with a sibling or relative you haven't seen for some time.

## Sunday 17th

There's a sentimental theme to your astrology and you might be looking to the past. You may be feeling emotional, whether you're missing someone or remembering good times past. Try and keep your feet on the ground and make sensible decisions. Let your head rule your heart.

## Monday 18th

You could win big today, perhaps via an inheritance or family wealth. If this is about your money, you may have proof that you recently made the right investment. Mercury remains on go slow until the beginning of January, so hold tight until then before you make your next big move.

## Tuesday 19th

Where do you find beauty in your life? It's an important question to ask today whether you require beauty in your immediate surroundings or beautiful connections in your life. You may be feeling wistful or sentimental and be aware of the close ties that bind you and the ones you love.

## Wednesday 20th

When it comes to love, be careful not to get carried away today. There's a hidden theme to relationships which hints at unpredictable or spontaneous happenings. Yes, it can be exciting, but anything goes. If you're at an office party, your inner hedonist could come out to play.

## Thursday 21st

Keep close tabs on spending in the run-up to the festive season. Get your family involved if you want to be careful about the cost of Christmas presents, for example. You could organise a gift exchange or cap a limit on how much you spend on one another.

. . . . . . . . . . . . . . . . . .

## Friday 22nd

The Sun's move into Capricorn today could shed a light on money and your financial situation. It may have been a big year for you and now's the time to prepare and look ahead. Take stock of what's worked out and what hasn't worked out. Make some firm plans for your future.

## Saturday 23rd

Communication planet Mercury retreats into your star sign today. You may need to be extra careful what you say over the festive season as your enthusiasm could be overpowering. You tend to have strong beliefs but that doesn't mean everyone is going to agree with you.

## Sunday 24th

It might be Christmas Eve, but you've got your sensible head on. You may be ready to let go of a financial or emotional tie that's past its sell-by date and could help you be better off in 2024. Today and tomorrow, the moon is in your relationship zone, so talk, be intimate and connect with your partner.

## Monday 25th

You'll have the best day if you put other people's needs before your own. This may sound strange on Christmas Day, but you might realise that someone in your life wants reassurance or a confidence boost. After all, the festive season is about honouring family and relational ties.

## Tuesday 26th

If you're harbouring feelings for someone you're not with over the festive break, you may be wise to keep this to yourself. Today could be punchy as everyone wants to get their voice heard. Let someone else step in to be a calming influence. For now, that's not your role.

## Wednesday 27th

Today's full moon is the perfect opportunity to make a big decision that could help stabilise you financially as you move into the new year. This decision might be linked to your home and family as the full moon takes place in Cancer, the family star sign, highlighting these key areas.

## Thursday 28th

Your end-of-year astrology is feisty and lively but potentially packed with good fortune. There could be news about money, a cash bonus or wealth flowing your way. Yet, as your planet Jupiter rules freedom, you may make a decision to move away from a materialistic lifestyle.

## Friday 29th

Lovely Venus is gracing your star sign during the end of year celebrations. This combination tends to mean you're more attractive to other people and popular too. Make a bid to get on the guest-list of your party of choice and actively seek joy and happiness in your life.

## Saturday 30th

As the year comes to a close, your ruling planet Jupiter turns direct and this is powerful for you. Whatever's been on hold in your life, it's the equivalent of the floodgates opening as fresh energy pours in. This might bring a new work opportunity your way or freedom from a stressful situation.

## Sunday 31st

There's a strong sense of give and take in your stars on the last day of 2023. You may be helping out someone close to you, or you receive a gift or offer of help yourself. The natural flow of money and caring works both ways. This is what will make your New Year's Eve special.

# Sagittarius

·················

## PEOPLE WHO SHARE
## YOUR SIGN

# PEOPLE WHO
# SHARE YOUR SIGN
· · · · · · · · · · · · · · · · ·

The free spirits of the zodiac can be easy to identify with their expansive thinking and lively approach to life. From Winston Churchill to Nicki Minaj, it feels like these inspiring Sagittarians were placed on Earth to motivate the masses. Whether this dual sign is influenced more by their intellectual mind or their physical strength, Sagittarians' daring attitudes will see them go far. Discover which of these optimistic Sagittarians share your exact birthday and see if you can spot the similarities.

## November 23rd
Alexis Ren (1996), Miley Cyrus (1992), Snooki (1987), Kelly Brook (1979), Zoë Ball (1970), Vincent Cassel (1966), Nicolás Maduro, Venezuelan President (1962), John Schnatter (1961), Ludovico Einaudi (1955)

## November 24th
Sarah Hyland (1990), Katherine Heigl (1978), Colin Hanks (1977), Stephen Merchant (1974), Shirley Henderson (1965), Billy Connolly (1942), Dale Carnegie (1888), Henri de Toulouse-Lautrec (1864)

## November 25th
Katie Cassidy (1986), Gaspard Ulliel (1984), Joel Kinnaman (1979), Christina Applegate (1971), John F. Kennedy Jr. (1960), Ben Stein (1944), Ricardo Montalbán (1920), Karl Benz (1844)

## November 26th

Rita Ora (1990), Danny Welbeck (1990), Tamsin Egerton (1988), Chris Hughes (1983), DJ Khaled (1975), Peter Facinelli (1973), Tina Turner (1939), Charles M. Schulz (1922)

## November 27th

Professor Green (1983), Robin Givens (1964), Yulia Tymoshenko, Ukrainian Prime Minister (1960), William Fichtner (1956), Jil Sander (1943), Manolo Blahnik (1942), Jimi Hendrix (1942), Bruce Lee (1940)

## November 28th

Karen Gillan (1987), Trey Songz (1984), Mary Elizabeth Winstead (1984), Daniel Henney (1979), Jon Stewart (1962), Martin Clunes (1961), Alfonso Cuarón (1961), Judd Nelson (1959), Ed Harris (1950), Friedrich Engels (1820)

## November 29th

Diego Boneta (1990), Lauren German (1978), Chadwick Boseman (1977), Anna Faris (1976), Ryan Giggs (1973), Don Cheadle (1964), Jacques Chirac, French President (1932), Jackie Stallone (1921), C. S. Lewis (1898)

## November 30th

Kaley Cuoco (1985), Chrissy Teigen (1985), Elisha Cuthbert (1982), Steve Aoki (1977), Ben Stiller (1965), Gary Lineker (1960), Billy Idol (1955), Ridley Scott (1937), Winston Churchill (1874), Lucy Maud Montgomery (1874), Mark Twain (1835)

## December 1st

Chanel Iman (1990), Zoë Kravitz (1988), Vance Joy (1987), Janelle Monáe (1985), Sarah Silverman (1970), Pablo Escobar (1949), Bette Midler (1945)

## December 2nd

Charlie Puth (1991), Alfred Enoch (1988), Teairra Marí (1987), Action Bronson (1983), Aaron Rodgers (1983), Britney Spears (1981), Nelly Furtado (1978), Lucy Liu (1968)

## December 3rd

Amanda Seyfried (1985), Dascha Polanco (1982), Jenna Dewan (1980), Holly Marie Combs (1973), Brendan Fraser (1968), Daryl Hannah (1960), Julianne Moore (1960), Ozzy Osbourne (1948)

## December 4th

Niykee Heaton (1994), Tyra Banks (1973), Kevin Sussman (1970), Jay-Z (1969), Fred Armisen (1966), Marisa Tomei (1964), Jeff Bridges (1949), Albert Bandura (1925)

## December 5th

Anthony Martial (1995), Frankie Muniz (1985), Ronnie O'Sullivan (1975), Paula Patton (1975), Eddie the Eagle (1963), King Bhumibol the Great of Thailand (1927), Walt Disney (1901), Werner Heisenberg (1901)

## December 6th

Stefanie Scott (1996), Alberto Contador (1982), Sarah Rafferty (1972), Judd Apatow (1967), Nick Park (1958), Peter Buck (1956), Agnes Moorehead (1900)

## December 7th

Nicholas Hoult (1989), Emily Browning (1988), Aaron Carter (1987), Dan Bilzerian (1980), John Terry (1980), Sara Bareilles (1979), Jennifer Carpenter (1979), Noam Chomsky (1928)

## December 8th

AnnaSophia Robb (1993), Amir Khan (1986), Nicki Minaj (1982), Ian Somerhalder (1978), Dominic Monaghan (1976), Sinéad O'Connor (1966), Teri Hatcher (1964), Kim Basinger (1953), John Banville (1945)

## December 9th

Simon Helberg (1980), Jesse Metcalfe (1978), Kurt Angle (1968), Felicity Huffman (1962), Donny Osmond (1957), John Malkovich (1953), Dame Judi Dench (1934), Kirk Douglas (1916)

## December 10th

Teyana Taylor (1990), Gonzalo Higuaín (1987), Kim Sears (1987), Raven-Symoné (1985), Emmanuelle Chriqui (1975), Susanna Reid (1970), Kenneth Branagh (1960), Michael Clarke Duncan (1957), Emily Dickinson (1830)

## December 11th

Hailee Steinfeld (1996), Mos Def (1973), Mo'Nique (1967), DJ Yella (1967), Marco Pierre White (1961), Nikki Sixx (1958), Jermaine Jackson (1954), Pranab Mukherjee, Indian President (1935)

## December 12th

Yuvraj Singh (1981), Mayim Bialik (1975), Mädchen Amick (1970), Jennifer Connelly (1970), Regina Hall (1970), Sheila E. (1957), Bill Nighy (1949), Frank Sinatra (1915), Edvard Munch (1863)

## December 13th

Katherine Schwarzenegger (1989), Taylor Swift (1989), Amy Lee (1981), Tom DeLonge (1975), Jamie Foxx (1967), Steve Buscemi (1957), Christopher Plummer (1929), Dick Van Dyke (1925)

## December 14th

Tori Kelly (1992), Vanessa Hudgens (1988), Michael Owen (1979), Miranda Hart (1972), Natascha McElhone (1969), Dilma Rousseff, Brazilian President (1947), Jane Birkin (1946), Stan Smith (1946), B. K. S. Iyengar (1918), King George VI of the United Kingdom (1895)

## December 15th

Jesse Lingard (1992), Keylor Navas (1986), Camilla Luddington (1983), Charlie Cox (1982), Michelle Dockery (1981), Adam Brody (1979), Don Johnson (1949), Tim Conway (1933), Gustave Eiffel (1832)

· · · · · · · · · · · · · · · · · ·

## December 16th

Zara Larsson (1997), Anna Popplewell (1988), Theo James (1984), Danielle Lloyd (1983), Krysten Ritter (1981), Miranda Otto (1967), Benjamin Bratt (1963), Philip K. Dick (1928), Wassily Kandinsky (1866)

## December 17th

Dynamo (1982), Katheryn Winnick (1977), Milla Jovovich (1975), Sarah Paulson (1974), Giovanni Ribisi (1974), Rian Johnson (1973), Eugene Levy (1946), Muhammadu Buhari, Nigerian President (1942), Pope Francis (1936)

## December 18th

Ashley Benson (1989), Christina Aguilera (1980), Katie Holmes (1978), Sia Furler (1975), DMX (1970), Brad Pitt (1963), Jonathan Cainer (1957), Ray Liotta (1954), Steven Spielberg (1946), Keith Richards (1943), J. J. Thomson (1856)

## December 19th

Alexis Sánchez (1988), Karim Benzema (1987), Jake Gyllenhaal (1980), Alyssa Milano (1972), Tyson Beckford (1970), Richard Hammond (1969), Jennifer Beals (1963), Til Schweiger (1963), Maurice White (1941), Édith Piaf (1915)

## December 20th

JoJo (1990), Bugzy Malone (1990), Bob Morley (1984), Jonah Hill (1983), Lara Stone (1983), Ashley Cole (1980), Chris Robinson (1966), Jenny Agutter (1952), Uri Geller (1946), Peter Criss (1945)

## December 21st

Steven Yeun (1983), Tom Payne (1982), Emmanuel Macron, French President (1977), Kiefer Sutherland (1966), Ray Romano (1957), Jane Kaczmarek (1955), Chris Evert (1954), Samuel L. Jackson (1948), Jane Fonda (1937), Phil Donahue (1935)